The Top Ten Guide to Paris™

By

Françoise Chaniac Dumazy

The Internationalist
96 Walter Street/Suite 200
Boston, MA 02131 USA

The Internationalist®

International Business, Investment and Travel

Managing Editor: Patrick W. Nee

Published by:
The Internationalist Publishing Company
96 Walter Street/Suite 200
Boston, MA 02131, USA
Tel: 617-354-7722
Publisher@internationalist.com

Photography by:
Cover photograph by Françoise Chaniac Dumazy

ISBN: 1-891382-04-7

Special Sales:
Books of the Internationalist Publishing Company are available for bulk
purchases at special discounts for sales promotions, corporate identity
programs or premiums. The Internationalist Publishing Company
publishes books on international business, investment and travel. For
further information contact the Special Sales department at: Special Sales,
The Internationalist, 96 Walter Street/Suite 200, Boston, MA 02131.

The Internationalist Publishing Company
96 Walter Street/Suite 200
Boston, MA 02131 USA
Tel: 617-354-7722
Sales@internationalist.com

e-mail: publisher@internationalist.com
web site: http://www.internationalist.com

Welcome to Paris.

Paris has been the inspiration of artists, writers and lovers for centuries and the sought after prize of Emperors, Generals and Kings. What a disappointment it would be to visit Paris and not experience the very best the city has to offer.

THE TOP TEN GUIDE TO PARIS is designed so you will experience the very best of Paris: the best restaurants, the best museums, the best sights and the best entertainment. THE TOP TEN GUIDE TO PARIS is the only guide you will need. Turn the pages as a knowledgeable Parisian guides you through the best of classic and contemporary Paris.

There is so much to Paris that you can get overwhelmed and miss some of the city's outstanding high points. Parisian Françoise Chaniac Dumazy makes sure you experience the city's crown jewels: the great museums, the dramatic panoramas, the romantic restaurants, the hot discos, and the classic Parisian cafes.

As a special feature Françoise has added the metro stations that take you directly to your destinations. Whether you are visiting for a few days or a few weeks, THE TOP TEN GUIDE TO PARIS lets you focus on the best of everything so that your Paris experience is a rich and rewarding one.

THE TOP TEN TRAVEL GUIDES are designed to meet the needs of today's sophisticated travelers. They highlight the best the world has to offer. They are available for other cities of the world. Just ask your bookseller.

Best wishes for a pleasant visit to Paris.

Françoise Chaniac Dumazy

Parisian Françoise Chaniac Dumazy knows Paris intimately and brings the city to life for readers in this dynamic guide. From her student days at the Ecole Supérieure de Commerce de Paris, in the heart of Paris, to her days as an analyst of international finance at JP Morgan, located at place Vendome, the luxury center of Paris, Françoise has recorded the best and most exciting of all that Paris has to offer. No one knows Paris like Françoise. Françoise knows the small cafés, the grand restaurants, the romantic rendezvous and the exciting discos. Françoise cuts through the clutter and delivers to you the very best of Paris so that your visit to Paris is the very best experience.

Contents

Top Ten Paris Basics

Experiencing Paris

Top Ten Paris Hotels

Top Ten Paris Restaurants and Cafés

About Food and Drink in Paris

Top Ten Shopping in Paris

Top Ten Arts & Entertainment in Paris

Top Ten Nightlife in Paris

Top Ten About Paris

Top Ten Business Life in Paris

Paris

THE TOP TEN GUIDE

The Top Ten Things to Know when Planning your Trip

1. **You need a passport (USA, Canada, and Australia citizens).**

2. **You don't need a visa, unless you intend to stay longer than 90 days in a row.**

3. **You don't need special shots.**

4. **By plane**
   Major airlines flying to Paris:
   - From US: American (800.433.7300), Continental (800.231.0856), Delta (800.211.1212), TWA (800.892.4141), United (800.241.65220) and Air France (800.237.2747).
   - From Canada: Air Canada (800 361.8620), Canadian Airlines (800.426.7000).
   - From the UK: British Airways (0181.897.4000), Air France (0181.759.2311), Virgin Atlantic and British Midlands.

   Airlines fly to two airports:
   - Orly, South of Paris
   - Roissy-Charles de Gaulle, North of Paris

5. **Via the Channel tunnel from the UK**
   Eurostar
   From the UK Ph: 0181.784.1333
   From France Ph: 01.42.66.40.43 - Fax: 01.44.51.6.02
   High speed train linking Paris and London in three hours.
   The Shuttle
   19 rue des Mathurins, Paris 9th
   Ph: 01.47.42.50.00
   For those who want to take their cars.

6. **By Ferry from the UK**
   Hoverspeed
   Ph: 03.21.46.14.14
   Speedy Seacats between Boulogne and Folkestone.
   Dealink or P&O Ferries
   Ph: 01.44.94.40.40 / 01.44.51.00.51
   1 1/2 hour ferry trip between Calais and Dover.

7. Climate
If you have the choice, the best months are certainly May, June, and September. Most Parisians leave the city in August for their annual vacations.

8. Electricity
France runs on 220V and outlets are different. You need to buy a converter, which costs about $20, as well as an adapter for French outlets. Adapters and converters can be found at the BHV department store, 52 rue de Rivoli, Paris 4th - métro: Hôtel de Ville.

9. Paris Tourist Office
127 av. des Champs-Elysées, Paris 8th - métro: Charles de Gaulle-Etoile
Ph: 01.49.52.53.54 - Fax: 01.49.52.53.00
Open daily from 9 am to 8 pm. Closed May 1.
Useful number for reserving hotels, sightseeing tours or for information on Paris. Be aware that during high season hotels are often full in Paris. Reservations are highly recommended.

10. Embassies
- United States
  2 rue Saint-Florentin, Paris 1st - métro: Concorde
  Ph: 01.40.39.84.11 / 01.43.12.12.12 in emergencies
  Open weekdays from 9 am to 4 pm.
- Canada
  35 av Montaigne, Paris 8th - métro: Franklin D. Roosevelt
  Ph: 01.44.43.29.16
  Open weekdays from 8.30 am to 11 am.
- Australia
  4 rue Jean-Rey, Paris 15th - métro: bir-Hakeim
  Ph: 01.40.59.33.00 / 01.40.59.33.01 in emergencies
  Open weekdays from 9 am to 5.30 pm.
- United Kingdom
  35 rue du Faubourg-St-Honoré, Paris 8th - métro: Madeleine
  Ph: 01.42.66.91.42
  Open weekdays from 9.30 am to 1 pm and 2.30 pm to 6 pm.

The Top Ten Things to Know for Getting around Paris

A few tips to help you move around in Paris.

I. From and to Roissy Charles de Gaulle airport

There are several ways to get to Paris center from Roissy airport:

- By bus (departure every 15 minutes / cost: between 40 and 55F): Air France buses (stop at Porte Maillot, not far from the Arc de Triomphe) or Roissy Bus (stop at Opéra).
- By train: use the RER line B (a one-way ticket costs 45F).
- By taxi: it costs about 200F.

2. From and to Orly airport

There are several ways to get to Paris center from Orly airport:

- By bus (departure every 15 minutes / cost: between 30 and 40F): Air France buses (stop at Invalides) or Orlybus (stop at Denfert-Rochereau).
- By train: take the Orlyval shuttle to Antony station, then the RER line B (a one-way ticket costs 50F).
- By taxi: it costs about 160F.

3. Métro:

The Métro: is the ideal way to get around Paris: 15 lines cover the city and nearby suburbs. Very regular and fast trains take you anywhere in minutes. Wherever you are in Paris you'll find a metro station at less than 5-minute walking distance.

4. Buses

Buses offer you a great view of the city. Some of the lines hit Paris' major sights:

- The bus No. 29, with its open back, goes from Gare St Lazare to the Bastille, going through Opéra, Pompidou and the Marais.
- The bus No. 72 follows the Seine, from Hôtel de Ville to Trocadéro.
- The bus No. 73 goes down the Champs-Elysées.

5. Taxis

There are about 14,900 taxis in Paris. Nevertheless, it is sometimes difficult to find one during peak time or late at night. Taxis with lit signs are not available. Rates are around 8F per kilometer. The two major companies are Taxi Bleus (01.49.36.10.10) and Taxi G7 (01.47.39.47.39). G7 taxis accept major credit cards for fares over 50F.

6. Driving in Paris

If you plan to stay only in Paris, do not take a car. Driving in Paris can easily become a nightmare, and parking will be even worse! If you plan to rent a car (it can be useful if you want to go outside the city), you should bring along an International Driving Permit (IDP). And be aware that the legal blood alcohol level for drivers is 0.5%, the equivalent of two glasses of wine.

Most major car-rental companies are represented in France at the airport or in the center of Paris:

- Avis   Ph: 01.46.10.60.60 - Fax: 01.46.21.65.60
- Budget   Ph: 01.46.86.65.65 - Fax: 01.46.86.22.17
- Hertz   Ph: 01.39.38.38.38 - Fax: 01.39.38.35.13

7. Telephones
Local Pay Phones

- If you want to make local telephone calls, you need to buy a calling card "50 or 120 calling units" at a tobacco shop, metro station or post office. You cannot use coins, pay phones no longer take coins. Calling cards only.

International Calls

- To phone abroad from France, dial 00+country code+local code+phone number. To call France from abroad, dial the international code+33+region code (1 for Paris skip the zero)+8-digit number.

Cellular Phones

- European cellular operators use a different technology than in North America. Thus, if you want or need to stay in touch while in Paris or anywhere in Europe, you will need to rent a GSM-900 phone from a specialized company in Europe.

- Rent A Cell Express (116,bis av. des Champs-Elysées, Paris 8th - Ph: 01.53.93.78.00 Fax: 01.53.93.78.09) provides a good service at attractive rates, and delivers and picks-up the phones at your convenience. You need reservations at least 24 hours in advance.

8. Arrondissements

Paris is divided up into 20 districts, called "arrondissements". The first eight arrondissements are the most central and contain most of the best sights. The last two digits of the zip code give the arrondissement (75011 is the eleventh arrondissement for instance).

9. River: left bank / right bank

When talking about a place or giving an address, the Parisians often refer to the right bank (rive droite) and the left bank (rive gauche) of the Seine. The "rive gauche" is the artistic and student area, including the Quartier Latin and St-Gemain-des-Prés, while the "rive droite" is more traditional and commercial; on that side you'll find the Marais, the Louvre, the Opéra neighborhoods and the Champs-Elysées.

10. French Floor Numbering System

The French floor system is different from the American one: in France the first floor corresponds to the second floor in the U.S.

- Street level (US)   Floor zero or "rez-de-chaussée"
- 2nd floor (US)   1st Floor - "premier étage"
- 3rd floor (US)   2nd floor - "deuxieme etage"
- Basement (US)   Basement - "sous-sol"

The Top Ten Things to Know about French Money

1. **The units of French currency** are the franc and the centime: 1 franc=100 centimes.

2. **Bills** are in denominations of 500, 200, 100, 50, and 20 francs.

3. **Coins** are 20, 10, 5, 2, 1 francs and 50, 20, 10, 5 centimes.

4. **ATMs** can be found everywhere in Paris and are the easiest way to get francs.

5. **The best exchange rates** are found at banks or ATMs. Avoid hotels, airports and other touristy places.

6. **Traveler's checks** may be exchanged at banks (they usually charge 1% or 2% commission) but you usually cannot use them to pay in stores.

7. **Most banks** are open Monday to Friday from 9 am to 12 pm and 2 pm to 5 pm, on Saturdays from 9 am to 12 pm.

8. **The Post Office** also exchanges foreign currency for French Francs (open Monday to Friday from 8 am to 7 pm and Saturday from 8 am to 12 pm).

9. **American Express office**
   11 rue Scribe, Paris 9th - <u>métro</u>: Opéra
   Ph: 01.47.77.70.07
   Open daily from 9 am to 6.30 pm. Closed on Sundays.

10. **Ruesch International**
    700 11th St. NW, 4th floor, Washington, DC 20001
    Ph: 800/424-2923
    For American citizens who need a check made out in French francs before leaving.

The Top Ten Emergency Telephone Numbers

A few telephone numbers and addresses to remember.

1. **SAMU (Ambulance)**
   Dial 15

2. **Police Headquarters**
   Dial 17 or 01.53.71.53.71 or 01.53.73.53.73

3. **Fire Department**
   Dial 18

4. **SOS Médecins (doctors who make home calls at any time)**
   Ph: 01.43.37.77.77 or 01.47.07.77.77

5. **Lost or stolen credit cards**
   Visa: 01.42.77.11.90
   Diner's Club: 01.47.62.75.75
   Eurocard / Mastercard: 01.45.67.53.53
   American Express: 01.47.77.72.00

6. **American Hospital of Paris (Hôpital Américain)**
   63 blvd Victor Hugo, 92200 Neuilly-sur-Seine
   Ph: 01.46.41.25.25 - Fax: 01.46.24.49.38
   24-hour English-speaking emergency service: 01.47.47.70.15

7. **Anti-Poison Center**
   Ph: 01.40.37.04.04

8. **Pharmacy**
   Swann Rocher Pharmacy
   6 rue de Castiglione, Paris 1st - <u>métro</u>: Tuileries
   Ph: 01.42.60.72.96 - Fax: 01.42.60.44.12
   Open daily from 9 am to 7.30 pm. Closed Sundays.
   The only pharmacy where your prescription in English will be translated so that the pharmacist can give you the equivalent.

9. Lost and Found

36 rue des Morillons, Paris 15th - <u>métro</u>: Convention
Ph: 01.55.76.20.00
Open Mondays, Wednesdays and Fridays from 8.30 am to 5 pm. Tuesdays and Thursdays from 8.30 am to 8 pm.

10. Vehicle breakdown

SOS dépannage 24h/24h
Ph: 01.47.07.99.99 - Fax: 01.47.07.21.04

The Top Ten Things to know about the Métro:

The Paris metro is the most efficient way to get around Paris. Wherever you are in Paris you'll be at less than 5 minutes walking distance from a metro station.

1. How to use it
Locate the departure station and the arrival station on your metro map. Check if they are on the same line; if they are, note the name of the last station on the line: it's the "direction" you have to follow. If you must change lines, check on the metro map at which station you must change; a connection is called "correspondance". "Sortie" means exit.

2. Hours
From 5.30 am to 1.00 am.

3. Frequency
You don't wait more than 5 minutes. During peak hours trains may arrive every two minutes.

4. Tickets validity
A single ticket is valid for any one-way journey on the metro system and within zones 1 & 2 of the RER.

5. Information
Information line: 08.36.68.77.14 from 6 am to 9 pm and 08.36.68.41.14 in English.

6. The RER (Réseau Express Régional)
The RER is a network of fast trains that link Paris and the surburbs. It's very convenient to reach an opposite destination within Paris (for instance from Gare de Lyon to Charles de Gaulle - Etoile). If you want to go outside Paris (outside zones 1 & 2) you need to buy a special ticket at the RER station.

7. Price
A metro ticket costs 8 francs. A "carnet" -10 tickets- costs 46 francs. If you plan to stay one week or one month, you can buy the weekly (75 francs) or the monthly (250 francs) ticket (which cannot be shared by different persons).

8. The "Paris Visite" ticket

Choose between the one-day, two-day, three-day or five-day unlimited travel tickets for the metro, bus and RER. They cost 50, 80, 110, and 170 francs, respectively, and give you discounts in most museums. Sale in the main metro/RER stations, airports, and the Paris Tourist Office.

9. Safety

The metro is relatively safe but you should be careful with your wallet because of frequent pickpocketing.

10. Metro entrances

At Abbesses station (18th arrondissement), note an example of the Art Nouveau metro entrances designed by Hector Guimard between 1898 and 1904.

The Top Ten Holidays

1. January 1
New Year's Day   Jour de l'an

2. March-April (Sun-Mon)
Easter   Pâques

3. May 1
Labor Day   Fête du Travail

4. May 8
Victory Day for World War II   Victoire 1945

5. May (Thur)
Ascension Day   L'Ascension

6. June (Sun-Mon)
Pentecost or Whit Sunday   Pentecôte

7. July 14
Bastille Day (National Day)   Fête Nationale

8. August 15
Assumption Day   L'Assomption

9. November 11
Veterans' Day   Le onze novembre

10. December 25
Christmas   Noël

The Top Ten Paris Historic Events

Here are the major Paris historic events from the Gallo-Roman era to the 20th century.

1. **300 B.C.**
   The "Parisii" settle down in the "Ile de la Cité".

2. **508 A.D.**
   Clovis chooses his capital in Paris.

3. **1180-1223**
   Philippe Auguste builds the Louvre and a great wall surronding Paris.

4. **1784-91**
   Building of the wall of "fermiers généraux" (on the site of today's border between Paris and the Suburbs).

5. **July 14, 1789**
   The Bastille prison is stormed. Beginning of French Revolution.

6. **1792**
   The Tuileries are stormed, the kingdom falls and the Republic is proclaimed.

7. **1793-94**
   Reign of Terror: Louis XVI and Marie-Antoinette are guillotined on place de la Concorde.

8. **1870-71**
   The Franco-Prussian war: Paris falls. The "Commune de Paris" is repressed by Versailles people during the bloody week in May 1971.

9. **June 1940**
   World War II; Paris is occupied by German armies.

10. **August 1944**
    Paris is liberated.

The Top Ten Must See Areas

There are some "classics" in Paris that you simply cannot miss if you want to discover the French capital.

1. Le Louvre

34-36 quai du Louvre, Paris 1st - <u>métro</u>: Palais Royal
Ph: 01.40.20.53.17 - Guided tours for individuals:
01.40.20.52.09 - Fax: 01.40.20.58.24
Mon & Wed 9 am to 9.45 pm / Thurs-Sun 9 am to 6 pm.
Closed on Tuesdays.
Former home of the French kings, the Louvre is now the largest museum in the world. It has been recently renovated, enlarged and embellished. You'll find magnificent collections of Oriental, Egyptian, Greek, Etruscan and Roman antiquities, French sculptures, objets d'art, French paintings and the paintings of the Northern Schools (including Rubens). Don't miss the most famous masterpieces: the Venus de Milo, the Victory of Samothrace and the Mona Lisa by Leonardo da Vinci.

2. Place des Vosges - Marais

Paris 4th - <u>métro</u>: Saint-Paul or Chemin-Vert
Inaugurated in 1612 as Place Royale, the Place des Vosges is the most elegant square in Paris, with its stylish red and white brick residences, its arcades and its lovely garden. It is located in the heart of the Marais, the oldest district in Paris, where you'll find splendid private mansions.

3. Notre-Dame

6 place du Parvis de Notre-Dame, Paris 4th - <u>métro</u>: Cité or St-Michel
Ph: 01.42.34.56.10 - Fax: 01.40.51.70.98
Open daily from 8 am to 7 pm. Closed on Saturdays from 12.30 pm to 2 pm.
Built between 1163 and 1345, Notre-Dame cathedral is a masterpiece of French Gothic art. It is located on the Ile de la Cité, where the Parisii first settled in the third century before Jesus Christ.

4. Ile Saint-Louis

Paris 4th - <u>métro</u>: Pont-Marie
The small Ile Saint-Louis is one of the most charming and romantic spots in Paris.

5. Quartier Latin

Paris 5th & 6th - métro: Saint-Michel, Odéon, Maubert-Mutualité, Jussieu or Cardinal-Lemoine

The Latin Quarter has a large population of students and academics. Among the prestigious institutions of higher education, you'll find the Sorbonne, the Collège de France, and the Ecole Normale Supérieure. This district has become more and more touristy over the past few years. Don't miss the lively Mouffetard street and the Contrescarpe square, the shop-lined boulevard St-Michel, and the romantic Jardin du Luxembourg.

6. Champs Elysées

Paris 8th - métro: Franklin D. Roosevelt or George V or Charles de Gaulle-Etoile

The world's most famous avenue has become very touristy. You still have a great perspective with the Louvre and place de la Concorde in the bottom and the Arche de la Défense behind the Arc de Triomphe.

7. Musée d'Orsay

1 rue de Bellechasse, Paris 7th - métro: Solférino or Rue du Bac
Ph: 01.40.49.48.14 - Fax: 01.45.48.21.23
Open daily from 10 am to 6 pm (9.15 pm on Thursdays). Closed on Mondays. During the summer the museum opens at 9 am.

The Orsay train station, inaugurated for the World Exhibition of 1900, was transformed into a museum devoted to the art of the second half of the 19th century.

8. Eiffel Tower

Champ de Mars, Paris 7th - métro: Bir-Hakeim
Ph: 01.44.11.23.23 - Fax: 01.44.11.23.22
Open daily from 9 am to 11 pm (to midnight in July and August)

While the public abhorred it upon its conception, it became the symbol of Paris and is now famous worldwide. From the top of the tower you have a great view over the capital.

9. Place Vendôme
Paris 1st - <u>métro</u>: Opéra or Tuileries
One of the most elegant squares in Paris, home to the most famous jewelry shops and to the Ritz hotel.

10. Montmartre and the Sacré-Coeur
From the <u>métro</u>: Anvers, climb the Montmartre hill to reach the basilica Sacré-Coeur and then the lively Place du Tertre filled with cafés, restaurants and portrait artists. A few blocks southwest, you'll find the famous red-light district, Pigalle, and along the boulevards de Clichy and de Rochechouart the famous cabarets and nightclubs, including the Moulin-Rouge.

The Top Ten Things to Do

If you want to discover Paris and Parisians and escape tourists' crowds, here are a few suggestions:

1. Spend a few hours in a very Parisian Café, on boulevard St-Germain.

2. Discover French food at one of the liveliest street markets on Rue Mouffetard (Paris 5th).

3. Eat ice cream at Berthillon, Paris' best ice cream shop, on Ile Saint-Louis.

4. Go window-shopping along the Faubourg St-Honoré and the Place Vendôme.

5. Have a rest in the Square du Vert-Galand, on the Ile de la Cité.

6. Around five o'clock, have a delicious pastry with tea in a very cozy "salon de thé" (tea-room) in the Marais.

7. Take a boat tour on the Seine at night.

8. Go to the ballet at Opéra Garnier.

9. Spend all your savings in one of most the famous restaurants to discover fine French cooking and flavorful wines.

10. On Sunday, go for a walk in Bois de Boulogne and discover where Parisian families spend their weekends and get a breath of fresh air.

The Top Ten Walks During the Day

Paris is the ideal city for walkers: walking in Paris is never boring; every 100-meters you discover an attractive building, a charming square or an old boutique. Some neighborhoods are particularly pleasant for strollers.

1. The Marais
The Marais is the most lively, charming and trendy neighborhood in Paris. It covers the 3rd and 4th arrondissements. Not to miss: the Jewish quarter around rue des Rosiers, the elegant place des Vosges, the gay district around the rue Vieille du Temple and rue Ste-Croix de la Bretonnerie, and the great rue des Francs-Bourgeois with its nice boutiques and restaurants.

2. Saint-Germain des Prés
The other trendy and pleasant district in Paris, frequented by students and artists. Not to miss: the charming place Saint-Sulpice and place de Furstenberg, the boulevard St-Germain and its famous cafés (Le Flore, Les Deux Magots) and chic boutiques, the rue Bonaparte and its art galleries, the rue Visconti and rue St-André-des-Arts.

3. Ile Saint-Louis and Ile de la Cité
Walk along the charming rue St-Louis-en-l'Ile, take the footbridge to the Ile de la Cité, and go through the small garden behind Notre-Dame. After visiting the two most beautiful churches in Paris, Notre-Dame and Sainte-Chapelle, go through the quiet place Dauphine and finally have a rest in the romantic Square du Vert-Galand.

4. Opéra, Palais Royal, Jardin des Tuileries and the Louvre
From the busy Opéra Garnier square, go down on the avenue de l'Opéra, take a left on the rue des Petits Champs (don't miss the Galerie Vivienne) until the beautiful place des Victoires, then go through the Jardins du Palais Royal and end in the newly embellished Jardins des Tuileries.

5. **Quartier Latin: rue Mouffetard, Panthéon, Jardin du Luxembourg**

   It's a pleasure to get lost among the narrow streets in the Latin Quarter, the centre of French intellectual life. Don't miss the Sorbonne, the labyrinth streets between the Seine and place Maubert, and the rue Mouffetard and rue de la Montagne-Ste-Geneviève behind the Panthéon. Finally, if you're tired, have a rest in the romantic Jardin du Luxembourg.

6. **Place Vendôme, Rue Royale, Rue du Faubourg-St-Honoré**

   Between the Place Vendôme, Madeleine and the Rond-Point des Champs-Elysées, there are some of the most chic streets in Paris. You'll find jewels around the place Vendôme, crystal and china on rue Royale and clothing on rue du Faubourg-St-Honoré.

7. **Champs-Elysées, Avenue Montaigne**

   From the Pont de l'Alma, walk on avenue Montaigne which houses the famous Haute Couture boutiques, then from Concorde, walk up on the Champs-Elysées, finally go to the top of the Arc de Triomphe from which you'll have a great view to the capital.

8. **Montmartre**

   The highest hill in Paris, site of the basilica Sacré-Coeur, has the atmosphere of a village. Rapidly escape from the very touristy square "du Tertre", and discover the picturesque streets: rue Junot, villa Léandre and rue des Saules, where you'll find the last remaining vineyard in Paris.

9. **Champ de Mars, Tour Eiffel, Trocadéro**

   A classic: after a walk through the Champ de Mars from where you can admire beautiful private houses, climb the Eiffel Tower for a nice view, then cross the river and reach the Trocadéro.

10. **Centre Pompidou, Les Halles**

    Don't miss the lively rue Montorgueil with its food market, the Eglise St-Eustache and the pleasant square behind the Halles, and of course the area around Centre Georges Pompidou with its street musicians and performers.

The Top Ten Romantic Spots in Paris

Is Paris the most romantic city in the world? Here are a few addresses to help you answer the question...

1. Square du Vert-Galand
Paris 1st - métro: Pont-Neuf
Very quiet and romantic garden at the tip of Ile de la Cité, offering a great view over the Seine.

2. Ile Saint-Louis
Paris 4th - métro: Pont-Marie
Very charming and romantic island in the heart of Paris.

3. Top of the Tour Eiffel at night
Champ de Mars, Paris 7th - métro: Bir-Hakeim
Ph: 01.44.11.23.23 - Fax: 01.44.11.23.22
Open daily from 9 am to 11 pm (to midnight in July and August)
For a very romantic evening, you can have dinner in Jules Verne restaurant, which serves excellent food.

4. Place des Vosges
Paris 4th - métro: Saint-Paul or Chemin-Vert
During the weekend many artists play music under the arcades surrounding the square, creating a great atmosphere.

5. Jardin du Luxembourg
Paris 6th - métro: Odéon or St-Michel or RER Luxembourg
One of the most romantic parks in Paris.

6. Place de Furstemberg
Paris 6th - métro: Mabillon
A very pretty square in the heart of the Latin Quarter.

7. Place du marché Sainte-Catherine
Paris 4th - métro: Saint-Paul
Very intimate square in the heart of the Marais, surrounded by restaurants.

8. Jardins des Tuileries

Paris 1st - <u>métro</u>: Tuileries or Concorde

Former royal garden when the Louvre was the home of French kings, the Jardins des Tuileries have recently been embellished and are very pleasant today. Nice view over the Louvre, place de la Concorde and Musée d'Orsay.

9. Pont des Arts

Built in 1804 and located next to the Louvre, this footbridge is a meeting spot for artists and painters.

10. Jardins du Palais Royal

Paris 1st - <u>métro</u>: Palais Royal-Musée du Louvre

Surrounded by beautiful covered galleries, this park was the site of many historical events.

The Top Ten Modern Architectural Sites

Built in the 1980s and 1990s, the Grande Arche de la Défense, the pyramides of the Louvre, the Opéra Bastille and the very new Bibliothèque Nationale were part of President Mitterrand's "grands projets". Some of them caused controversy.

1. Centre Georges Pompidou
19 rue Beaubourg, Paris 4th - <u>métro</u>: Châtelet Les Halles
Ph: 01.44.78.12.33
More than 600 architects from around the world competed to work on President Pompidou's project to build a huge art center in Paris. The Italian Piano and the British Rogers were chosen finally. The very modern building, made of metal, glass and pipes was finished in 1977 and was very controversial among Parisians; some of them were horrified! Today it is one of the most visited places in Paris. It houses the National Museum of Modern Art, the Public Information Library, the Institute of Acoustic and Musical Research and the Department for Cultural Development. Due to extensive renovation works the center is closed from October 1997 to December 1999.

2. Institut du Monde Arabe
1 rue des Fossés Saint-Bernard, Paris 5th - <u>métro</u>: Jussieu, Cardinal-Lemoine or Sully-Morland
Ph: 01.40.51.38.38 - Fax: 01.43.54.76.45
Open daily from 10 am to 6 pm. Closed on Mondays.
Conceived by Jean Nouvel, this beautiful building contains an array of Arab-Islamic art, textiles, and ceramics.

3. La Grande Arche de la Défense
1 parvis de la Défense, 92040 Paris la Défense - <u>métro</u>:,
La Défense
Ph: 01.49.07.27.57 - Fax: 01.49.07.27.90
Open daily from 10 am to 7 pm
Officially opened in 1989, it holds special events and temporary exhibitions.

4. Opéra Bastille
Place de la Bastille, Paris 12th - <u>métro</u>: Bastille
Ph: 01.40.01.17.89 - Fax: 01.40.01.16.16
Inaugurated in 1989, this opera house is one of the most modern in the world.

5. Bibliothèque Nationale de France (National Library)
Quai François Mauriac, Paris 13th - <u>métro</u>: Quai de la gare
Ph: 01.53.79.59.59
Open daily from 10 am to 7 pm, Sundays from 12 pm to 6 pm.
Closed on Mondays.
Conceived by François Mitterrand, the new national library has been inaugurated in 1997: four modern buildings that look like books standing open. With its 395 km of shelves, it is one of the largest libraries in the world.

6. Pyramides du Louvre
Conceived by the architect Peï, the striking all-in-glass pyramid now has its "sister", the reversed pyramid inside the commercial gallery of Carroussel du Louvre.

7. La Géode (Cité des Sciences et de l'Industrie)
30 av. Corentin Cariou, Paris 19th - <u>métro</u>: Porte de la Villette
Ph: 08.36.68.29.30
Open daily from 10 am to 6 pm (7 pm on Sundays). Closed on Mondays.
The Geode is a modern cinema with hemispheric screen (movie every hour from 10 am to 9 pm).

8. Parc André Citroën
Paris 15th - <u>métro</u>: Balard
Futuristic park with varied gardens, waterfalls, sculptures.

9. Tour Montparnasse
33 av. du Maine, Paris 15th - <u>métro</u>: Montparnasse-Bienvenüe
Ph: 01.45.38.52.56
The tallest office building (210 meters / 690 feet) from which one has a great view.

10. Les colonnes du Buren (Palais Royal)
Paris 1st - <u>métro</u>: Palais-Royal
These striped columns inside the park of the Palais Royal may disappoint you. When constructed, they were the subject of great debate among Parisians.

The Top Ten Museums

If you plan to visit many museums and monuments, you can buy the "Carte Musées et Monuments", a card which gives you free entry to 65 important venues in Paris. The cost for 1/3/5 days is 70/140/200 francs. It is available from the venues or tourist offices.

1. Musée du Louvre

34-36 quai du Louvre, Paris 1st - <u>métro</u>: Palais Royal
Ph: 01.40.20.53.17 - Guided tours for individuals:
01.40.20.52.09 - Fax: 01.40.20.58.24
Mon & Wed 9 am to 9.45 pm / Thurs-Sun 9 am to 6 pm.
Closed on Tuesdays.
Former home of the French kings, the Louvre is now the largest museum in the world. It has been recently renovated, enlarged and embellished. You'll find magnificent collections of Oriental, Egyptian, Greek, Etruscan and Roman antiquities, French sculptures, objets d'art, French paintings and the paintings of the Northern Schools (including Rubens). Don't miss the most famous masterpieces: the Venus de Milo, the Victory of Samothrace and the Mona Lisa by Leonardo da Vinci.

2. Musée d'Orsay

1 rue de Bellechasse, Paris 7th - <u>métro</u>: Solférino or Rue du Bac
Ph: 01.40.49.48.14 - Fax: 01.45.48.21.23
Open daily from 10 am to 6 pm (9.15 pm on Thursdays).
Closed on Mondays. During the summer the museum opens at 9 am.
The Orsay train station, inaugurated for the World Exhibition of 1900, was transformed into a museum devoted to the artistic creation of the second half of the 19th century. Masterpieces by Van Gogh (L'Eglise d'Auvers-sur-Oise), Monet (Nymphéas bleus), Renoir and Cézanne.

3. **Musée National d'Art Moderne - Centre Georges Pompidou**

19 rue Beaubourg, Paris 4th - <u>métro</u>: Châtelet Les Halles
Ph: 01.44.78.12.33

The National Museum of Modern Art houses famous paintings by Kandinsky, Delaunay, Klee, Miro, Dali, among many others. Due to extensive renovation works the Centre Georges Pompidou is closed from October 1997 to December 1999.

4. **Musée Picasso**

Hôtel de Juigné - Salé
5 rue de Thorigny, Paris 3rd - <u>métro</u>: Saint-Paul or Chemin-Vert
Ph: 01.42.71.25.21 - Fax: 01.48.04.75.46
Open daily from 9.30 am to 6 pm (5.30 pm from October to March). Closed on Tuesdays.

In the heart of the Marais, exceptional collection of Picasso's paintings and sculptures.

5. **Musée Rodin**

Hôtel Biron
77 rue de Varenne, Paris 7th - <u>métro</u>: Varenne
Ph: 01.44.18.61.10 - Fax: 01.45.51.17.52
Open daily from 9.30 am to 5.45 pm (4.45 pm from October to March). Closed on Mondays.

One of the most beautiful museums in Paris which houses all the most famous works by the sculptor Auguste Rodin.

6. **Cité des Sciences et de l'Industrie La Villette**

30 av. Corentin Cariou, Paris 19th - <u>métro</u>: Porte de la Villette
Ph: 08.36.68.29.30
Open daily from 10 am to 6 pm (7 pm on Sundays). Closed on Mondays.

This center presents the great technological achievements.

- *Explora: permanent exhibitions on the earth and the universe, languages and communication, technological and industrial developments.*
- *The Planetarium.*
- *The children's city and the techno city: play areas and interactive areas for children.*
- *The Geode: cinema with hemispheric screen (every hour from 10 am to 9 pm).*
- *Cinaxe: an earth-shaking experience (every 15 minutes from 11 am to 6 pm).*

7. Grand Palais

3 av. du Général Eisenhower, Paris 8th - <u>métro</u>: Champs-
Elysées-Clémenceau or Franklin-Roosevelt
Ph: 01.44.13.17.17 - Fax: 01.45.63.54.33
Open daily from 10 am to 8 pm (10 pm on Wednesdays).
Closed on Tuesdays.
Prestigious temporary exhibitions.

8. Musée Carnavalet

23 rue de Sévigné, Paris 3rd - <u>métro</u>: Saint-Paul
Ph: 01.42.72.21.13
Open daily from 10 am to 5.40 pm. Closed on Mondays.
*Located in two beautiful private mansions in the Marais, this
museum describes the history of Paris through splendid
collections.*

9. Musée National d'Histoire Naturelle

Jardin des Plantes
57 rue Cuvier, Paris 5th - <u>métro</u>: Jussieu or Gare d'Austerlitz
Ph: 01.40.79.30.00 - Fax: 01.40.79.34.84
Open daily from 10 am to 6 pm (10 pm on Thursdays). Closed
on Tuesdays.
*Don't miss the newly renovated "Grande Galerie de
l'Evolution", with impressive zoological collections.*

10. Institut du Monde Arabe

1 rue des Fossés Saint-Bernard, Paris 5th - <u>métro</u>: Jussieu,
Cardinal-Lemoine or Sully-Morland
Ph: 01.40.51.38.38 - Fax: 01.43.54.76.45
Open daily from 10 am to 6 pm. Closed on Mondays.
*The Institute of the Arab World contains a beautiful array of
Arab-Islamic art, textiles, and ceramics from the 7th to the
19th century. Restaurant and terrace on the 9th floor with a
great view over Paris.*

The Top Ten Small Museums

Paris houses numerous small museums dedicated to one artist or one type of art. Some of them are outstanding.

1. Musée Marmottan Claude Monet
2 rue Louis-Boilly, Paris 16th - <u>métro</u>: La Muette
Ph 01.42.24.07.02 - Fax: 01.40.50.65.84
Open daily from 10 am to 5.30 pm. Closed on Mondays.
Masterpieces by Claude Monet and other Impressionist paintings (Gauguin, Renoir, Sisley).

2. Musée de l'Orangerie
Place de la Concorde, Paris 1st - <u>métro</u>: Concorde
Ph: 01.42.97.48.16 - Fax: 01.42.61.30.82
Open daily from 9.45 am to 5.15 pm. Closed on Tuesdays.
Houses the famous Nymphéas by Claude Monet.

3. Musée Jacquemart-André
158 blvd Haussmann, Paris 8th - <u>métro</u>: Miromesnil
Ph: 01.42.89.04.91 - Fax: 01.42.25.09.23
Open daily from 10 am to 6 pm.
Exceptional art collection of Edouard André and Nélie Jacquemart in their private mansion (Italian renaissance and 18th century French paintings). Very pleasant restaurant.

4. Musée de l'Armée - Hôtel des Invalides
Esplanade des Invalides - <u>métro</u>: Latour Maubourg or Varenne
Ph: 01.44.42.37.72 - Fax: 01.44.42.37.64
Open daily from 10 am to 6 pm (5 pm from October to March).
Houses a collection of weapons and uniforms of the French army. The Eglise du Dôme houses the tomb of Napoléon 1st.

5. Musée des Arts et Traditions Populaires
Bois de Boulogne
6 av. du Mahatma Gandhi, Paris 16th - <u>métro</u>: Sablons
Ph: 01.44.17.60.00 - Fax: 01.44.17.60.60
Open daily from 9.30 am to 5 pm. Closed on Tuesdays.
French customs, beliefs and way of life throughout the ages.

6. Musée National du Moyen-Age, Thermes de Cluny

6 place Paul-Painlevé, Paris 5th - <u>métro</u>: Cluny, Saint-Michel or Odéon
Ph: 01.53.73.78.00 - Fax: 01.46.34.51.75
Open daily from 9.15 am to 5.45 pm. Closed on Tuesdays.
Medieval art.

7. Musée National Eugène Delacroix

6 rue de Furstemberg, Paris 6th - <u>métro</u>: Saint-Germain-des-Prés
Ph: 01.44.41.86.50 - Fax: 01.43.54.36.70
Open daily from 9.30 am to 12 pm and 1.30 pm to 5 pm.
Closed on Tuesdays.
Paintings and personal items of Delacroix in his studio on Furstemberg square.

8. Musée de la Mode et du Textile

Palais du louvre
107 rue de Rivoli, Paris 1st - <u>métro</u>: Palais-Royal
Ph: 01.44.55.57.50 - Fax: 01.44.55.57.93
Open daily from 11 am to 6 pm (until 10 pm on Wednesdays), Saturdays and Sundays from 10 am to 6 pm. Closed on Mondays.
Exceptional collection of costumes from the 17th to the 20th century.

9. Musée de la Marine

Palais de Chaillot
Place du Trocadéro, Paris 16th - <u>métro</u>: Trocadéro
Ph: 01.53.65.6.69 - Fax: 01.53.65.69.65
Open daily fron 10 am to 6 pm. Closed on Tuesdays.
Maritime history from the 18th century to today.

10. Musée National Gustave Moreau

14 rue de la Rochefoucault, Paris 9th - <u>métro</u>: Trinité
Ph: 01.48.74.38.50 - Fax: 01.48.74.18.71
Open daily from 10 am to 12.45 pm and 2 pm to 5.15 pm, Mondays and Wednesdays from 11 am to 5.15 pm. Closed on Tuesdays.
Home and studio of the symbolist painter Gustave Moreau.

The Top Ten Art Galleries

The avenue Matignon (right bank) and the rue des Beaux Arts (left bank) are the two main locations for art galleries.

I. Galerie Claude Bernard
5-7 rue des Beaux-Arts, Paris 6th - <u>métro</u>: St-Germain-des-Prés
Ph: 01.43.26.97.07
Open daily from 9.30 am to 12.30 pm and 2.30 pm to 6.30 pm.
Closed Sundays, Mondays.
Splendid gallery with works by Bacon, Monnard, Botero, Giacometti.

2. Galerie Lelong
13 rue de Téhéran, Paris 8th - <u>métro</u>: Franklin D. Rossevelt
Ph: 01.45.63.13.19
Open daily from 10.30 am to 6 pm, Saturdays 2 pm to 6.30 pm. Closed Sundays, Mondays.
One of the most important galleries in Paris. Works by great 20th century artists: Giacometti, Miró, Alechinsky, James Brown, and Stenberg.

3. Galerie Louise Leiris
47 rue de Monceau, Paris 8th - <u>métro</u>: Monceau
Ph: 01.45.63.20.56
Open daily from 10 am to 12 pm and 2:30 pm to 6 pm. Closed Sundays, Mondays.
Not to be missed gallery with works by Picasso, Léger, Braque, Masson, Laurens, and others.

4. Galerie Schmit
396 rue St-Honoré, Paris 1st - <u>métro</u>: Concorde
Ph: 01.42.60.36.36
Open daily from 9 am to 12.30 pm and 2 pm to 6.30 pm.
Closed Saturdays, Sundays.
Works by great artists of the 19th and 20th century: Delacroix, Chagall, Dufy, Utrillo and many others.

5. Artcurial
9 av. Matignon, Paris 8th - <u>métro</u>: Franklin D. Rossevelt
Ph: 01.42.99.16.04 - Fax: 01.43.59.29.81
Open daily from 10.30 am to 7.15 pm. Closed Sundays, Mondays.
Works by Arman, Laurens, Miró, de Chirico, and Zadkine.

6. Galerie Pilzer

16 av. Matignon, Paris 8th - <u>métro</u>: Miromesnil
Ph: 01.43.59.90.07
Open daily from 10 am to 7 pm. Closed Sundays.
Works by painters and sculptors of the 20th century: Picasso, Chagall, Frank Stella, Jean Helion.

7. Bernheim Jeune

83 rue du Faubourg St-Honoré, Paris 8th - <u>métro</u>: Champs-Elysées-Clémenceau
Ph: 01.42.66.60.31
and 27 av. Matignon, Paris 8th - <u>métro</u>: Franklin D. Rossevelt
Ph: 01.42.66.65.03
Open daily from 10.30 am to 12.30 pm and 2.30 pm to 6.30 pm. Closed Sundays, Mondays.
Works by Monet and Pissaro.

8. Didier Imbert Fine Arts

19 av. Matignon, Paris 8th - <u>métro</u>: Miromesnil
Ph: 01.45.62.10.40
Open daily from 10 am to 1 pm and 2.30 pm to 7 pm. Closed Sundays.
Works by Botero, Wesselmann, Brauner, Brancusi.

9. Galerie Berggruen

70 rue de l'Université, Paris 7th - <u>métro</u>: Solférino
Ph: 01.42.22.02.12
Open daily from 10 am to 1 pm and 2.30 pm to 7 pm. Closed Sundays, Mondays.
Collection of modern classics: Dali, Klee, Masson, Matisse, Miró, and Pissaro.

10. Galerie Marwan Hoss

12 rue d'Alger, Paris 1st - <u>métro</u>: Tuileries
Ph: 01.42.96.37.96
Open daily from 9.30 am to 12.30 pm and 2 pm to 6.30 pm. Closed Sundays.
Works by Matisse, Bonnard, Calder, Giacometti.

The Top Ten Private Mansions in the Marais

At the beginning of the 17th century the Marais became the heart of Paris. It is now home to beautiful private mansions dating from the 16th to 18th century, some of which can be visited.

I. Hôtel Carnavalet

23 rue de Sévigné, Paris 3rd - <u>métro</u>: Saint-Paul
Ph: 01.42.72.21.13 - Fax: 01.42.72.01.61
Open daily from 10 am to 5.40 pm. Closed on Mondays.
This renaissance private mansion houses the Carnavalet museum.

2. Hôtel de Sully

62 rue Saint-Antoine, Paris 4th - <u>métro</u>: Saint-Paul
Ph: 01.44.61.20.00 - Fax: 01.44.61.21.81
Open daily from 8 am to 7 pm.
Parisian home of the Duke of Sully, this beautiful mansion now houses the National Society of Historical monuments and sites.

3. Hôtel de Sens

1 rue du Figuier, Paris 4th - <u>métro</u>: Saint-Paul
Ph: 01.42.78.14.60 - Fax: 01.42.78.22.59
Open daily from 1.30 pm to 8 pm, Saturday from 10 am to 8.30 pm. Closed on Sundays and Mondays.
Beautiful building dating from the middle-ages.

4. Hôtel de Soubise

60 rue des Francs-Bourgeois, Paris 3rd - <u>métro</u>: Hôtel-de-Ville
Ph: 01.40.27.60.96 - Fax: 01.40.27.66.45
Open daily from 12 pm to 5.45 pm, Saturdays and Sundays from 1.45 pm to 5.45 pm. Closed on Tuesdays.
Houses the National Archives and French history museum.

5. Hôtel de Rohan

87 rue Vieille-du-Temple, Paris 3rd - <u>métro</u>: Saint-Paul or Hôtel-de-Ville
Ph: 01.40.27.60.96 - Fax: 01.40.27.66.45

6. Hôtel Salé
5 rue de Thorigny, Paris 3rd - <u>métro</u>: Saint-Paul or Chemin-Vert
Ph: 01.42.71.25.21 - Fax: 01.42.71.12.99
Houses the Picasso museum.

7. Hôtel de Guénégaud des Brosses
60 rue des Archives, Paris 3rd - <u>métro</u>: Rambuteau or Hôtel-de-Ville
Ph: 01.42.72.86.43 - Fax: 01.42.77.45.70
Houses the Hunting and Nature museum.

8. Hôtel Hénault-de-Cantorbe
5/7 rue de Fourcy, Paris 4th - <u>métro</u>: Saint-Paul
Ph: 01.44.78.75.00 - Fax: 01.44.78.75.15
Houses the "European Photography Centre".

9. Hôtel de Lamoignon
24 rue Pavée, Paris 4th - <u>métro</u>: Saint-Paul
Ph: 01.44.59.29.40 - Fax: 01.42.74.03.16
Houses Paris' huge history library.

10. Hôtel de Saint-Aignan
71 rue du Temple, Paris 3rd - <u>métro</u>: Temple
Ph: 01.40.29.94.65 - Fax: 01.40.29.07.45
Will house the Judaïsm art and history museum in 1998.

The Top Ten Historic Places Related to Artists

If you want to immerse yourself in the lives of Victor Hugo, Honoré de Balzac, Eugène Delacroix or other famous artists, visit where they lived, painted or wrote.

1. Maison Victor Hugo
6 place des Vosges, Paris 4th - <u>métro</u>: Saint-Paul or Bastille
Ph: 01.42.72.10.16 - Fax: 01.42.72.06.64
Open daily from 10 am to 5.40 pm. Closed on Mondays.
Victor Hugo lived here from 1832 to 1848. His home was transformed into a museum in 1902. You'll find souvenirs of his family, literary and political life.

2. Maison de Balzac
47 rue Raynouard, Paris 16th - <u>métro</u>: Passy or La Muette
Ph: 01.42.24.56.38 - Fax: 01.45.25.19.22
Open daily from 10 am to 5.40 pm. Closed on Mondays.
Honoré de Balzac's home was transformed into a museum, which displays his personal belongings (paintings, manuscripts).

3. Musée National Eugène Delacroix
6 rue de Furstemberg, Paris 6th - <u>métro</u>: Saint-Germain-des-Prés
Ph: 01.44.41.86.50 - Fax: 01.43.54.36.70
Open daily from 9.30 am to 12 pm and 1.30 pm to 5 pm.
Closed on Tuesdays.
Paintings and personal items of Delacroix in his studio at Furstemberg square.

4. Musée Zadkine
100 bis rue d'Assas, Paris 6th - <u>métro</u>: Notre-Dame-des-Champs or Vavin
Ph: 01.43.26.91.90
Open daily from 10 am to 5.30 pm. Closed on Mondays.
Home and studio of the Russian sculptor Ossip Zadkine.

5. Musée National Gustave Moreau

14 rue de la Rochefoucault, Paris 9th - <u>métro</u>: Trinité
Ph: 01.48.74.38.50 - Fax: 01.48.74.18.71
Open daily from 10 am to 12.45 pm and 2 pm to 5.15 pm,
Mondays and Wednesdays from 11 am to 5.15 pm. Closed on
Tuesdays.
Home and studio of the symbolist painter Gustave Moreau.

6. Closerie des Lilas

171 blvd du Montparnasse, Paris 6th - <u>métro</u>: Port-Royal
Ph: 01.43.54.21.68
*Many writers spent long hours talking, reading and writing in
this café, including Baudelaire, Verlaine, Gide, Apollinaire. It
was also a favorite of Ernest Hemingway and F. Scott
Fitzgerald.*

7. 24 rue Visconti

Paris 6th - <u>métro</u>: St-Germain-des-Prés
Jean Racine lived here.

8. 19 quai Malaquais

Paris 6th - <u>métro</u>: St-Germain-des-Prés
Anatole France lived here.

9. 15/19 quai Malaquais

Paris 6th - <u>métro</u>: St-Germain-des-Prés
George Sand lived here.

10. 2 blvd Beaumarchais

Paris 11th - <u>métro</u>: Bastille
Beaumarchais lived here from 1732 to 1729.

The Top Ten Places Related to French History

Many buildings and squares in Paris were the scene of the capital's historic events.

1. Place de la Concorde
<u>Métro</u>: Concorde
Execution of Louis XVI and Marie-Antoinette in 1793 during the Reign of Terror.

2. Place de la Bastille
<u>Métro</u>: Bastille
The Bastille prison was stormed by a Parisian mob on 14 July 1789: it was the beginning of the French Revolution. The Reign of Terror followed.

3. Hôtel des Invalides - Musée de l'armée (military museum)
Esplanade des Invalides, Paris 7th - <u>métro</u>: Latour-Maubourg or Varenne
Ph: 01.44.42.37.67
Open daily from 10 am to 6 pm (5 pm from October to March)
The Hôtel des Invalides was commissioned by Louis XIV to house wounded soldiers. Napoléon's tomb is housed in the Eglise du Dôme.

4. La Conciergerie
Blvd du Palais, quai de l'Horloge - <u>métro</u>: Cité
Ph: 01.53.73.78.50 - Fax: 01.40.51.70.36
April-Sept: open daily from 9.30 am to 6 pm; Oct-March: open daily from 10 am to 4.30 pm.
A magnificent example of the architecture of the 14th century, the Conciergerie was the prison where Marie-Antoinette was kept during the French Revolution.

5. Le Louvre
34-36 quai du Louvre, Paris 1st - <u>métro</u>: Palais-Royal
Ph: 01.40.20.53.17
Former home of the French kings until Louis XIV decided to move to Versailles.

6. Place des Vosges
Métro: Saint-Paul or Chemin-Vert
Inaugurated in 1612 as the royal square.

7. Palais Royal
Métro: Palais-Royal
Housed young king Louis 14th in the 1640s.

8. L'Arc de Triomphe de l'Etoile
Paris 8th - métro: Charles de Gaulle - Etoile
This colossal Triumphal Arch was planned by Napoléon to celebrate his successes.

9. Panthéon
Place du Panthéon, Paris 5th - métro: Cardinal-Lemoine, Maubert-Mutualité or RER Luxembourg
Open from 9.30 am to 6.30 pm (10 am to 5.30 pm from October to March)
Since the French Revolution, the Panthéon has housed the ashes of the "great citizens of France", including Voltaire, Rousseau, Victor Hugo, Jean Moulin, André Malraux...

10. Musée Carnavalet
23 rue de Sévigné, Paris 3rd - métro: St-Paul
Ph: 01.42.72.21.13
Open daily from 10 am to 5.40 pm. Closed on Mondays.
Located in two beautiful private mansions in the Marais, this museum describes the history of Paris through splendid collections.

The Top Ten Gardens to See

There are many small gardens and parks inside the capital.
But if you really need a breath of fresh air, you'd better go to the
Bois de Boulogne or Bois de Vincennes at the periphery of Paris.

I. Jardin du Luxembourg
Paris 6th - <u>métro</u>: Odéon or St-Michel or RER Luxembourg
One of the most romantic parks in Paris.

2. Jardins des Tuileries
Paris 1st - <u>métro</u>: Tuileries or Concorde
Former royal garden when the Louvre was French kings'
home, the Jardins des Tuileries have just been embellished and
are very pleasant today. Nice view over the Louvre, place de la
Concorde and Musée d'Orsay.

3. Bois de Boulogne
Paris 16th - <u>métro</u>: Porte Maillot, Porte Dauphine or Porte
d'Auteuil
With 35 km of footpaths, 8 km of cyclepaths and 29 km of
bridleways, the Bois de Boulogne is the largest park in Paris.
After boating on Lac Inférieur, don't miss the fantastic flower
collection of the Parc de Bagatelle.

4. Jardin du Palais Royal
Paris 1st - <u>métro</u>: Palais Royal-Musée du Louvre
Surrounded by beautiful covered galeries, this park was the
site of many historical events.

5. Parc Montsouris
Paris 14th - RER Cité Universitaire or <u>métro</u>: Porte d'Orléans
Charming garden with its artificial lake, caves and waterfalls.

6. Parc des Buttes Chaumont
Paris 19th - <u>métro</u>: Buttes-Chaumont
Bordered by rues de Crimée, Manin and Botzaris, Paris 19th -
<u>métro</u>: Buttes-Chaumont
Nice lake overlooked by a promontory.

7. Parc Monceau

Paris 17th - <u>métro</u>: Monceau
In the heart of one of the most elegant residential districts.

8. Jardin des Plantes

Paris 5th - <u>métro</u>: Jussieu, Monge or Gare d'Austerlitz
Houses over 10,000 varieties of plants.

9. Jardin du Champ-de-Mars

Paris 7th - <u>métro</u>: Ecole Militaire or RER Champ-de-Mars
Designed to enhance the Eiffel Tower. Large lawns open to the public.

10. Bois de Vincennes

Paris 12th - <u>métro</u>: Chateau de Vincennes, Porte Dorée, Porte de Charenton or Liberté
Another very large park in the southeast of Paris. Houses a zoo.

The Top Ten Bridges

Paris without its bridges would not be Paris! All the important architectural sites are situated around the Seine and its 36 bridges.

1. **Pont-Neuf**
   The oldest (built in the 16th century) and the most famous bridge in Paris. Very present in the French movie "Les Amants du Pont-Neuf".

2. **Pont Alexandre III**
   Inaugurated for the World Exhibition of 1900, this heavy bridge with angels and gold horses is the most extravagant bridge in Paris.

3. **Pont des Arts**
   Built in 1804 and located next to the Louvre, this footbridge is a meeting spot for artists and painters.

4. **Pont de l'Archeveché**
   Beautiful view over the cathedral Notre-Dame.

5. **Pont Saint-Louis**
   Footbridge linking the two islands Ile de la Cité and Ile Saint-Louis.

6. **Pont Bir-Hakeim**
   Beautiful view over the Eiffel Tower.

7. **Pont de la Concorde**
   Splendid view over the Place de la Concorde.

8. **Pont Mirabeau**
   Immortalized by the French poet Apollinaire.

9. **Pont Royal**
   One of the oldest bridges in Paris, along with Pont-Neuf.

10. **Pont de la Tournelle**
    Pleasant view over Notre-Dame and Ile St-Louis.

The Top Ten Fountains

At one time, Paris had over 20,000 thousands fountains. Here are the most dramatic ones still remaining:

1. **Fontaine Stravinsky**
   Place Igor Stravinsky (beside the Centre Pompidou) Paris 4th - <u>métro</u>: Les Halles
   Fanciful and colorful fountains created by Jean Tinguely and Niki de Saint-Phalle.

2. **Fontaine des Innocents**
   Square des Innocents, Paris 1st - <u>métro</u>: Châtelet-Les Halles
   Designed by Pierre Lescot and sculptured by Jean Goujon, it's a chef-d'oeuvre of the Renaissance period.

3. **Fontaine de la Croix-du-Trahoir**
   Rue St-Honoré & Rue de l'Arbre Sec, Paris 1st - <u>métro</u>: Louvre-Rivoli

4. **Fontaine de la Place de la Concorde**
   Place de la Concorde, Paris 8th - <u>métro</u>: Concorde

5. **Fontaine de l'Observatoire**
   Avenue de l'Observatoire - RER Port-Royal or <u>métro</u>: Vavin
   Famous for the four parts of the world sculptured by Carpeaux.

6. **Fontaine Saint-Michel**
   Place St-Michel, Paris 6th - <u>métro</u>: St-Michel

7. **Fontaine de Médicis - Jardin du Luxembourg**
   Jardin du Luxembourg - RER Luxembourg or <u>métro</u>: St-Michel

8. **Fontaine des Quatre Evèques**
   Place St-Sulpice, Paris 6th - <u>métro</u>: Saint-Sulpice

9. **Fontaine Molière**
   Rue Richelieu & rue Molière, Paris 1st - <u>métro</u>: Palais-Royal
   Visconti built this foutain near the house where Molière died.

10. **Fontaine du Châtelet**
    Place du Châtelet, Paris 1st - <u>métro</u>: Châtelet

The Top Ten Covered Arcades - "Passages couverts"

Built at the beginning of the 19th century, these iron-and-glass covered arcades, which housed shops, restaurants, and theatres, were part of the social life. While many were demolished or fell into disrepair during the 20th century, some of them have been rescued and refurbished.

1. Galerie Véro-Dodat (1826)
19 rue Jean-Jacques Rousseau, Paris 2nd - <u>métro</u>: Palais-Royal
The most beautiful gallery with very nice boutiques.

2. Galerie Vivienne (1823)
4 rue des Petits-Champs, Paris 2nd - <u>métro</u>: Bourse
Built in 1823, it is today one of the most lively galleries.

3. Passage Choiseul (1827)
23 rue des Augustins, Paris 2nd - <u>métro</u>: Quatre-Septembre
The writer Louis-Ferdinand Céline lived there when he was a child; he gives a dark description of it in "Mort à crédit".

4. Passage des Panoramas (1800)
11 blvd Montmartre, Paris 2nd - <u>métro</u>: Rue-Montmartre
First "passage couvert" in Paris, described by Zola in his novel "Nana".

5. Galerie Colbert (1826)
6 rue Vivienne, Paris 2nd - <u>métro</u>: Bourse

6. Passage Jouffroy (1845)
10 blvd Montmartre, Paris 2nd - <u>métro</u>: Rue-Montmartre
First heated gallery in Paris.

7. Passage Verdeau (1847)
6 rue de la Grange-Bateliere, Paris 9nd - <u>métro</u>: Richelieu-Drouot or Le Pelletier
You'll find antiques and old books.

8. Passage du Grand-Cerf (1825)
145 rue Saint-Denis, Paris 4th - <u>métro</u>: Etienne Marcel

---

9. Passage Brady
18 rue du Faubourg-Saint-Denis, Paris 9th - <u>métro</u>:
Strasbourg-Saint-Denis

10. Passage du Caire
Rue du Caire, Paris 2nd - <u>métro</u>: Réaumur-Sebastopol or
Sentier

The Top Ten Squares

Each Parisian district has its own square and each square has its own story...

I. **Place des Vosges**
   Paris 4th - métro: Saint-Paul or Chemin-Vert
   The most elegant square in Paris with its red and white brick residences and its stylish garden. Inaugurated in 1612 as the royal square.

2. **Place Vendôme**
   Paris 1st - métro: Opéra or Tuileries
   Built during the reign of Louis XIV, this magnificent square now hosts the most famous jewelry shops and the Ritz hotel, Europe's most somptuous hotel.

3. **Place de la Concorde**
   Paris 8th - métro: Concorde
   Beautiful square where many important historic events occurred, including the execution of Louis XVI. A 3,300 year-old Egyptian obelisk stands at its center.

4. **Place de la Bastille**
   Paris 12th - métro: Bastille
   Site of the 1789 revolution.

5. **Place des Victoires**
   Paris 2nd - Métro: Palais-Royal or Bourse
   Superb square with its matching facades designed in 1685 by Versailles architect Hardouin-Mansart. Now home to many fashion boutiques.

6. **Place Dauphine**
   Paris 1st - métro: Pont-Neuf
   A very charming and quiet square which used to be an important royal square.

7. **Place du Marché Sainte-Catherine**
   Paris 4th - métro: Saint-Paul.
   Very intimate square in the heart of the Marais, surrounded by restaurants.

8. Place de Furstemberg
Paris 6th - <u>métro</u>: Mabillon
A very pretty square in the heart of the Latin Quarter.

9. Place du Tertre
Paris 18th - <u>métro</u>: Anvers or Abesses
The main square of the village of Montmartre, filled with cafés, restaurants and portrait artists.

10. Place du Palais-Royal
Paris 1st - <u>métro</u>: Palais-Royal
Borders on the Royal Palace gardens and the Comédie-Française.

The Top Ten Panoramas

Many rooftops of Paris offer beautiful views over the city and its monuments both day and night.

1. Tour Eiffel
Champ de Mars, Paris 7th - <u>métro</u>: Bir-Hakeim
Ph: 01.44.11.23.23 - Fax: 01.44.11.23.22
Open daily from 9 am to 11 pm (to midnight in July and August).
Spectacular view from the top of Paris' most famous monument. You can take the lift or the stairs up to the 2nd level and another lift takes you up to the 3rd level (top).

2. Tour Montparnasse
33 av. du Maine, Paris 15th - <u>métro</u>: Montparnasse
Ph: 01.45.38.52.56
Great view from Paris' tallest office building (210 meters / 690 feet).

3. Towers of Notre-Dame
Place du Parvis Notre-Dame, Paris 4th - <u>métro</u>: Cité
Ph: 01.42.34.56.10
Open daily from 9.30 am to 6.30 pm (5 pm from mid-September to March).
Exceptional view of the heart of Paris.

4. Dôme du Sacré Coeur
35 rue du Chevalier-de-la-Barre, Paris 18th - <u>métro</u>: Anvers
Ph: 01.42.51.17.02
Open daily from 9 am to 7 pm (6 pm in winter).
Panoramic view over the capital from the top of the basilica. From the parvis of the Basilica, you also have a great view on Parisian monuments.

5. Arc de Triomphe
Place Charles de Gaulle-Etoile - <u>métro</u>: Charles de Gaulle-Etoile
Ph: 01.43.80.31.31
Open daily from 9.30 am to 6 pm (Apr-Sept), from 10 am to 5.30 pm (Oct-Mar).
Great view over the Champs-Elysées.

6. Centre Georges-Pompidou (5th floor terrace)
Métro: Les Halles
The terrace remains open during the restoration work.

7. La Samaritaine (Store 2's terrace)
19 rue de la Monnaie, Paris 1st - métro: Pont-Neuf
Ph: 01.40.41.20.20
Open daily from 9.30 am to 7 pm. Closed on Sundays.
Beautiful view of the Conciergerie, Notre-Dame and the Pont-Neuf.

8. Le Printemps
64 blvd Haussmann, Paris 9th - métro: Havre-Caumartin
Ph: 01.42.82.57.87
Open daily from 9.35 am to 7 pm (10 pm on Thursdays).
Closed on Sundays.
From the terrace of the department store, there is a great view over the Opéra Garnier, Montmartre and Madeleine church.

9. Institut du Monde Arabe (9th floor terrace)
1 rue des Fossés-St-Bernard, Paris 5th - métro: Jussieu or
Cardinal Lemoine
Ph: 01.40.51.38.38
Open daily from 10 am to 6 pm. Closed on Mondays.
Panoramic view over Notre-Dame, Ile Saint-Louis and Ile de la Cité.

10. La Grande Arche de la Défense
Métro: La Défense
Ph: 01.49.07.27.57
Open daily from 10 am to 7 pm.
Beautiful view over La Défense area.

The Top Ten Churches

✗ 1. **Notre-Dame de Paris**

6 place du Parvis de Notre-Dame, Paris 4th - <u>métro</u>: Cité or St-Michel

Ph: 01.42.34.56.10 - Fax: 01.40.51.70.98

Open daily from 8 am to 7 pm. Closed on Saturdays from 12.30 pm to 2 pm.

Built between 1163 and 1345, Notre-Dame cathedral is a masterpiece of French Gothic art.

✗ 2. **La Sainte Chapelle**

4 blvd du Palais, Paris 1st - <u>métro</u>: Cité

Ph: 01.53.73.78.50 - Fax: 01.40.51.70.36

Open daily from 9.30 am to 6.30 pm from April to September, 10 am to 4.30 pm from October to March.

Located within the Paris law courts, Sainte-Chapelle is a pearl of gothic art. Many concerts take place here.

3. **Basilique du Sacré-Coeur**

Place St-Pierre, Paris 18th - <u>métro</u>: Anvers

Ph: 01.53.41.89.00 - Fax: 01.53.41.89.10

Open daily from 6.45 am to 11 pm.

This byzantine style basilica is Montmartre's best known monument.

4. **Saint-Etienne-du-Mont**

1 rue St-Etienne-du-Mont, Paris 5th - <u>métro</u>: Cardinal-Lemoine

Ph: 01.43.54.11.79 - Fax: 01.43.25.38.49

Open daily from 8 am to 12 pm and 2 pm to 7.30 pm, Sundays from 9 am to 12 pm and 2.30 pm to 7.30 pm. Closed on Mondays, July and August.

Lovely church which houses the remains of Sainte-Geneviève, the patron saint of Paris. Don't miss its graceful rood screen and its carved wooden pulpit.

5. **Basilique Saint-Denis**

Place de l'Hôtel-de-ville, St-Denis - <u>métro</u>: St-Denis-Basilique

Ph: 01.48.20.02.47

The burial place for many French kings, including Catherine de Médicis, Marie Antoinette and Louis XIV.

6. La Madeleine

Place de la Madeleine, Paris 8th - métro: Madeleine
Ph: 01.44.51.69.00 - Fax: 01.40.07.03.91
Open daily from 7 am to 7 pm, Sundays from 7 am to 1.30 pm
and 3.30 pm to 7 pm.
At the request of Napoleon 1st, it was built as a replica of a greco-roman temple.

7. Saint-Eustache

2 rue du Jour, Paris 1st - métro: Les Halles
Ph: 01.42.36.31.05
Nice example of Gothic art.

8. Saint-Germain-des-Prés

3 place St-Germain-des-Prés, Paris 6th - métro: St-Germain-des-Prés
Ph: 01.43.25.41.71
The oldest Roman church in Paris.

9. Saint-Séverin

1 rue des Prêtres St-Séverin, Paris 5th - métro: St-Michel
Ph: 01.43.25.96.63
Free concerts often performed on Sundays.

10. Saint-Sulpice

Place St-Sulpice, Paris 6th - métro: St-Sulpice
Ph: 01.46.33.21.78
Half-hour organ concerts on Sundays at 11.30 am.

The Top Ten Things To Do with Children

Paris and its suburbs offer plenty of attractions for children.

1. La Vilette - La Cité des Enfants

Cité des Sciences et de l'Industrie, Parc de la Villette
30 av Corentin-Cariou, Paris 19th - <u>métro</u>: Porte de la Villette
Ph: 01.40.05.70.00
Open daily from 10 am to 6 pm. Closed on Mondays.
A part of the Cité des Sciences et de l'Industrie is specially dedicated to children. 90-minute "discovery" programs are held every day. Fun experiments to discover the human body, the weather, the world of animals...

2. Musée National d'Histoire Naturelle (Museum of Natural History)

Jardin des Plantes
36 rue Geoffroy St-Hilaire, Paris 5th - <u>métro</u>: Gare d'Austerlitz or Censier-Daubenton
Ph: 01.40.79.30.00
Open daily from 10 am to 6 pm. Closed on Tuesdays.
Don't miss the newly renovated "Grande Galerie de l'Evolution", with impressive zoological collections.

3. Eurodisney

Marne-la-Vallée-Chessy (RER line A4) - 32 km east of Paris
Information by phone in France: 01.60.30.60.30, in the UK: 01733-335 567, or in the USA: 1-407-WDISNEY.
Open daily from 9 am to 8 pm during the week, from 9 am to 11 pm Saturdays and Sundays.

4. Jardin du Luxembourg

Paris 6th - <u>métro</u>: Cluny-la-Sorbonne or RER Luxembourg
Pony rides, toy sailboats and puppet shows.

5. Jardin des Tuileries

Paris 1st - <u>métro</u>: Tuileries or Concorde
Pony rides, toy sailboats and puppet shows.

6. Parc Astérix

30km north of Paris
Ph: 01.44.62.34.44
Open daily, from April to September, from 10 am to 6 pm.

From October to March open on Wednesdays, Saturdays and Sundays only.
Come and discover Astérix and Obélix, the heroes of the most famous French comic strip.

7. Palais de la Découverte

Av. Franklin D. Roosevelt, Paris 8th - métro Franklin-Roosevelt
Ph: 01.40.74.80.00 - Fax: 01.40.74.81.81
Open daily from 9.30 am to 6 pm and Sundays 10 am to 7 pm. Closed on Mondays.
The ancestor of the Cité des Sciences et de l'Industrie. Although a little old-fashioned, it's still very interesting.

8. Musée Grévin

10 blvd Montmartre, Paris 9th - <u>métro</u>: Rue-Montmartre
Ph: 01.47.70.85.05- Fax: 01.47.70.06.53
Open every day from 1 pm (10 am during school holidays) to 7 pm.
A wax museum with famous figures, from François Mitterrand to Claudia Schiffer.

9. Zoo

Parc zoologique de Paris
Bois de Vincennes
53 av.de St-Maurice, Paris 12th - <u>métro</u>: Porte-Dorée or Château-de-Vincennes
Ph: 01.44.75.20.00
Open daily from 9 am to 6.30 pm (5 pm from October to April).

10. Bois de Boulogne, Jardin d'Acclimatation

Paris 16th - <u>métro</u>: Sablons, Porte Maillot, la Muette or Porte d'Auteuil
A very nice place for the whole family to go canoeing, sunbathe or have a picnic in summer. There is also an amusement park for kids.

The Top Ten Seasonal Events

Many festivals are held in Paris between May and August.

1. Last Sunday of January - Salon des Antiquaires au Carroussel du Louvre
Carroussel du Louvre, 99 rue de Rivoli, Paris 1st - <u>métro</u>: Palais-Royal
Ph: 01.47.03.34.36
Extraordinary antiques to admire or to buy.

2. End April-beg. May - Foire de Paris
Parc des Expositions, Porte de Versailles, Paris 15th - <u>métro</u>: Porte de Versailles
Ph: 01.49.09.60.00
You'll find everything, from crafts to food and wines.

3. End of May - French Open of Tennis at Rolland Garros stadium
French Tennis Federation
2 av. Gordon-Bennett, Paris 16th
Ph: 01.47.43.48.00
Top international tennis championship.

4. Beg. June - Course des Garçons de Café
Departure and arrival at Hôtel-de-ville, Paris 1st - <u>métro</u>: Hôtel-de-Ville
Ph: 01.42.96.60.75
Famous race of professional waiters carrying trays of bottles and glasses.

5. June 21 - Fête de la Musique and Summer Solstice celebration
Streets of Paris
Ph: 01.40.03.94.70
Live music is performed throughout the streets, cafés and squares of Paris during all night.

6. Late June - Fête du Cinéma
During this special day, with one regular-price ticket you can see as many as movies you want.

7. Mid-June - mid-July - Festival du Marais

Tickets at: 44 rue François-Miron, Paris 4th - <u>métro</u>: Saint-Paul

Ph: 01.48.87.60.08

Classical and Jazz music, dance and theater are performed in the churches and historic hotels of the Marais.

8. 14th of July - Bastille Day

Celebrates the storming of the Bastille prison in 1789. Military parade along the Champs-Elysées in the morning; fireworks at night and firemen's balls in every arrondissement.

9. 4th Sunday of July - End of Tour de France

End of the world's most famous bicycle race on the Champs-Elysées.

10. 3rd Thursday of November - Le Beaujolais Nouveau

Cafés and restaurants celebrate the release of the season's new Beaujolais wine. Wine bars are overcrowded for this special evening.

The Top Ten Bus / Boat Tours

If you want to start your visit of Paris by a sightseeing tour, by boat or by bus, here are the best addresses.

1. **Cityrama**
   4 place des Pyramides, Paris 1st - <u>métro</u>: Pyramides
   Ph: 01.44.55.61.00 - Fax: 01.42.60.33.71
   Two-hour bus tours of the city, one-day trips around Paris (Versailles, Chartres...).

2. **Parisbus - Les Cars Rouges**
   Ph: 01.42.30.55.50 - Fax: 01.42.30.55.76
   Departure at Tour Eiffel.
   Two-hour tours in London-style double-decker buses, with stops at Trocadéro, Tour Eiffel, Champ-de-Mars, Musée du Louvre, Notre-Dame, Musée d'Orsay, Opéra, Champs-Elysées-Etoile, Grand-Palais.

3. **Paris Vision**
   214 rue Rivoli, Paris 1st - <u>métro</u>: Tuileries
   Ph: 01.42.60.30.01 - Fax: 01.42.86.95.36

4. **Touringscope**
   11 bis blvd Haussmann, Paris 9th - <u>métro</u>: Chaussée d'Antin or Richelieu-Drouot
   Ph: 01.53.34.11.91 - Fax: 01.53.34.11.90
   Guided tours including the visit of monuments.

5. **Balabus**
   RATP (the company which manages the metro, bus and RER network)
   Ph: 08.36.68.41.14 (in English)
   On Sundays and holidays from noon to 9 pm, the RATP runs a bus line, the Balabus, which starts at La Défense or Gare de Lyon and stops at all bus stops with sign "BB-BALABUS". It goes through all major sights of the city.

6. Vedettes du Pont-Neuf

Square du Vert-Galant - <u>métro</u>: Pont-Neuf
Ph: 01.53.00.98.98 - Fax: 01.40.26.38.98
One-hour boat excursions. Departures every 30 minutes in summer; every 45 minutes in winter.

7. Bateaux-mouches

Pont de l'Alma - <u>métro</u>: Alma-Marceau
Ph: 01.42.25.96.10
One-hour cruises, lunch and dinner cruises.

8. Bateaux parisiens

Notre-Dame: quai de Montebello - <u>métro</u>: St-Michel
Ph: 01.43.26.92.55
Tour Eiffel: port de la Bourdonnais - <u>métro</u>: Trocadéro
Ph: 01.44.11.33.44 - Fax: 01.45.56.07.88

9. Batobus

Tour Eiffel - Musée d'Orsay - Institut de France (opposite the Louvre) - Notre-Dame - Hôtel-de-Ville
Ph: 01.44.11.33.44
From Mid-April to October, the Batobus river shuttle docks at these five stops, every 35 minutes from 10 am to 7 pm.

10. Canauxrama

13 quai de la Loire, Paris 19th - <u>métro</u>: Jaurès
Ph: 01.42.39.15.00 - Fax: 01.42.39.11.24
From March to October, barges travel along the charming Canal Saint Martin and Canal de l'Ourcq.

The Top Ten Bike Rentals

Exploring Paris by bike is the ideal way to discover the charming corners of the capital, provided you are very careful of the crazy Parisian drivers!

I. Paris Vélo Rent a Bike
24 rue du Fer-à-Moulin, Paris 5th - <u>métro</u>: Censier-Daubenton
Ph: 01.43.37.59.22
Bilingual bicycle tours.

2. Paris à vélo, c'est sympa
9 rue Jacques Coeur, Paris 4th - <u>métro</u>: Bastille
Ph: 01.48.87.60.01
Holland-style bikes for 95F a day, 160F a weekend. Runs guided tours about 2.30 hours (Paris insolite, Coeur de Paris, Paris Contraste).

3. La maison du vélo
11 rue Fénélon, Paris 10th - <u>métro</u>: Gare du Nord
Ph: 01.42.81.24.72
The manager, Scott Inman, is American. Bike rental for 150F a day, 575F a weekend, racks and locks included.

4. Paris by Cycle
78 rue de l'Ouest, Paris 14th - <u>métro</u>: Pernety
Ph: 01.42.63.36.63
Bilingual bicycle tours.

5. Blue Marble Travel
4 rue Dussoubs, Paris 2nd - <u>métro</u>: Réaumur-Sébastopol
Ph: 01.42.36.02.34

6. VTT Center
1 place de Rungis, Paris 13th - <u>métro</u>: Tolbiac
Ph: 01.45.65.49.89

7. Mountain Bike Trip
Ph: 01.09.21.14.59 (voice mail)
Tours in English.

8. Vélo Cité

95 rue St-Dominique, Paris 7th - <u>métro</u>: Latour-Maubourg
Ph: 01.45.55.03.48

9. Métro: Bike

1 blvd Edgar Quinet, Paris 14th - <u>métro</u>: Edgar Quinet
Ph: 01.43.21.88.38

10. ACL

10 bis av. Grande Armée, Paris 17th - <u>métro</u>: Argentine
Ph: 01.47.66.19.19

The Top Ten Premium Hotels

Paris has some of the most elegant hotels in the world. They are pricey but worth the experience if you can afford it.

1. Hôtel Ritz
15 place Vendôme, Paris 1st - <u>métro</u>: Opéra
Ph: 01.43.16.30.30 or 800/448-8355 in North America - Fax: 01.43.16.36.68
One of the most luxurious hotels in the world.

2. Hôtel de Crillon
10 place de la Concorde, Paris 8th - <u>métro</u>: Concorde
Ph: 01.44.71.15.00 or 800/241-3333 in North America - Fax: 01.44.71.15.02
On Concorde square, a 200-year-old building which used to be the palace of the Duc de Crillon.

3. Plaza Athénée
23-27 av. Montaigne, Paris 8th - <u>métro</u>: Franklin D. Roosevelt
Ph: 01.53.67.66.65 or 800/448-8355 in North America - Fax: 01.53.67.66.66

4. George V
31 av. George V, Paris 8th - <u>métro</u>: George V
Ph: 01.47.23.54.00 or 800/225-5843 in North America - Fax: 01.47.20.40.00

5. Hôtel Meurice
228 rue de Rivoli, Paris 1st - <u>métro</u>: Tuileries or Concorde
Ph: 01.44.58.10.10 or 800/325-3535 - Fax: 01.44.58.10.15

6. Pavillon de la Reine
28 place des Vosges, Paris 3rd - <u>métro</u>: Bastille
Ph: 01.42.77.96.40 - Fax: 01.42.77.63.06
A charming hotel which faces the most elegant square.

7. Prince de Galles
33 av. George V, Paris 8th - <u>métro</u>: George V
Ph: 01.53.23.77.77 or 800/323-3535 in North America - Fax: 01.53.23.78.78

8. Lutetia

45 blvd Raspail, Paris 6th - <u>métro</u>: Sèvres-Babylone
Ph: 01.49.54.46.46 or 800/888-4747 in North America - Fax:
01.49.54.46.00

9. Royal Monceau

37 av. Hoche, Paris 8th - <u>métro</u>: Hoche
Ph: 01.42.99.88.00 - Fax: 01.42.99.89.90

10. Hôtel Balzac

6 rue Balzac, Paris 8th - <u>métro</u>: George V
Ph: 01.45.61.97.22 or 800/457-4000 in North America - Fax:
01.42.25.24.82

7000,08

The Top Ten Hotels (Medium Priced)

Paris also has many affordable hotels with a lot of charm and class. Expect to spend between 400F and 800F for a double room.

1. Hôtel des Grandes Ecoles
74 rue du Cardinal Lemoine, Paris 5th - <u>métro</u>: Cardinal-Lemoine or Monge
Ph: 01.43.26.79.23 - Fax: 01.43.25.28.15
Very charming hotel with its lovely garden and its small courtyard.

2. Hôtel des Marronniers *Visa 5-18-01*
21 rue Jacob, Paris 6th - <u>métro</u>: St-Germain-des-Prés
Ph: 01.43.25.30.60 - Fax: 01.40.46.83.56
A lot of charm. One takes one's breakfast in a lovely small garden.

3. Hôtel de l'Abbaye Saint-Germain
10 rue Cassette, Paris 6th - <u>métro</u>: St-Sulpice
Ph: 01.45.44.38.11
A very cozy and romantic place, near the St-Sulpice square.

4. Hôtel Saint-Germain
88 rue du Bac, Paris 7th - <u>métro</u>: Rue-du-Bac
Ph: 01.45.48.62.92 - Fax: 01.45.48.26.89
Conveniently located.

5-20-01

5. Grand Hôtel Malher
5 rue Malher, Paris 4th - <u>métro</u>: Saint-Paul
Ph: 01.42.72.60.92 - Fax: 01.42.72.25.37

6. Hôtel du 7e Art *144548500*
20 rue Saint-Paul, Paris 4th - <u>métro</u>: Saint-Paul
Ph: 01.42.77.04.03 - Fax: 01.42.77.69.10
Movie theme decorated.

7. Hôtel de Saint-Germain
50 rue du Four, Paris 6th - <u>métro</u>: Mabillon
Ph: 01.45.48.91.64
In a nice old private mansion.

8. Hôtel de Lutèce

65 rue St-Louis-en-l'Ile, Paris 4th - <u>métro</u>: Pont-Marie
Ph: 01.43.26.23.52 - Fax: 01.43.29.60.25

9. Hôtel du Quai Voltaire

19 quai Voltaire, Paris 7th - <u>métro</u>: Rue-du-Bac
Ph: 01.42.61.50.91 - Fax: 01.42.61.62.26
Known for its illustrious guests, including Wagner, Baudelaire, Oscar Wilde and Pissaro.

10. Hôtel Londres St-Honoré

13 rue Saint-Roch, Paris 1st - <u>métro</u>: Tuileries
Ph: 01.42.60.15.62 - Fax: 01.42.60.16.00
A conveniently located hotel with a very friendly staff.

The Top Ten Hotels (Inexpensive)

Here are the best addresses in the heart of Paris for budget travelers (between 200F and 400F a double room).

1. Hôtel de l'Espérance
15 rue Pascal, Paris 5th - <u>métro</u>: Censier-Daubenton
Ph: 01.47.07.10.99 - Fax: 01.43.37.56.19
Elegant rooms, professional staff.

2. Hôtel du Palais Bourbon
49 rue de Bourgogne, Paris 7th - <u>métro</u>: Varenne
Ph: 01.47.05.29.26 - Fax: 01.45.55.20.21
Pleasant rooms, welcoming staff and TV with CNN.

3. Familia Hôtel
11 rue des Ecoles, Paris 5th - <u>métro</u>: Jussieu or Maubert-Mutualité or Cardinal-Lemoine
Ph: 01.43.54.55.27 - Fax: 01.43.29.61.77
Attractive and friendly; nice view from the 5th and 6th floors.

4. Hôtel du Globe
15 rue des Quatre-Vents, Paris 6th - <u>métro</u>: Odéon
Ph: 01.43.26.35.50 - Fax: 01.46.33.17.29
Charming hotel in a nice building.

5. Grand Hôtel Léveque
29 rue Cler, Paris 7th - <u>métro</u>: Ecole Militaire or Latour-Maubourg
Ph: 01.47.05.49.15 - Fax: 01.45.50.49.36
Very close to the Eiffel tower and newly renovated.

6. Hôtel Malar
29 rue Malar, Paris 7th - <u>métro</u>: Latour-Maubourg
Ph: 01.45.51.38.46 - Fax: 01.45.55.20.19

7. Hôtel Vivienne
40 rue Vivienne, Paris 2nd - <u>métro</u>: Rue-Montmartre or Richelieu-Drouot or Bourse.
Ph: 01.42.33.13.26 - Fax: 01.40.41.98.18
Rooms have been recently renovated.

8. Grand Hôtel Jeanne d'Arc
3 rue de Jarente, Paris 4th - <u>métro</u>: St-Paul
Ph: 01.48.87.62.11 - Fax: 01.48.87.37.31
Quiet and charming hotel, very near the lovely
Marché- Ste-Catherine Square.

9. Hôtel Sévigné
2 rue Malher, Paris 4th - <u>métro</u>: St-Paul
Ph: 01.42.72.76.17 - Fax: 01.42.78.68.26

10. Hôtel - résidence Orsay
93 rue de Lille, Paris 7th - <u>métro</u>: Assemblée Nationale or
Solférino
Ph: 01.47.05.05.27 - Fax: 01.47.05.29.48
Very nice for the price! Closed in August.

The Top Ten Charming Small Hotels

Small hotels are often very charming and romantic, ideal for honeymooners. Make reservations because they are often full, especially during the high season.

1. Hôtel des Deux Iles
59 rue Saint-Louis-en-l'Ile, Paris 4th - <u>métro</u>: Pont-Marie
Ph: 01.43.26.13.35 - Fax: 01.43.29.60.25
Small but very pretty rooms in the heart of the Ile Saint-Louis. Very chic.

2. Hôtel de Nice (23 rooms)
42 bis rue de Rivoli, Paris 4th - <u>métro</u>: Hôtel-de-ville
Ph: 01.42.78.55.29 - Fax: 01.42.78.36.07
Elegance and refinement.

3. Hôtel Esmeralda (19 rooms)
4 rue Saint-Julien-le-Pauvre, Paris 5th - <u>métro</u>: St Michel
Ph: 01.43.54.19.20, Fax: 01.40.51.00.68
A very romantic hotel with a magnifique view of Notre-Dame. Reserve in advance since its reputation is known worldwide.

4. Hôtel Saint-Louis Marais
1 rue Charles V, Paris 4th - <u>métro</u>: Bastille or Sully Morand
Ph: 01.48.87.87.04 - Fax: 01.48.87.33.26
Closed in August.
Romantic hotel in the heart of the prettiest district in Paris.

5. Hôtel Saint-Merry (12 rooms)
78 rue de la Verrerie, Paris 4th - <u>métro</u>: Hôtel-de-Ville or Châtelet
Ph: 01.42.78.14.15 - Fax: 01.40.29.06.82
A former presbytery with gothic furniture in all rooms.

6. Hôtel les Degrés de Notre-Dame (10 rooms)
10 rue des Grands-Degrés, Paris 5th - <u>métro</u>: Maubert-Mutualité
Ph: 01.43.25.88.38 - Fax: 01.40.46.95.34
Ask for a room with a view on Notre-Dame.

7. Hôtel de la Place des Vosges (16 rooms)
12 rue de Birague, Paris 4th - <u>métro</u>: Saint-Paul or Bastille
Ph: 01.42.72.60.46 - Fax: 01.42.72.02.64

8. Hôtel Ermitage (12 rooms)
24 rue Lamarck, Paris 18th - <u>métro</u>: Lamarck-Caulaincourt
Ph: 01.42.64.79.22 - Fax: 01.42.64.10.33
Charming small hotel behind the Basilica of Sacré-Coeur.

9. Hôtel Le Pavillon (18 rooms)
54 rue Saint-Dominique, Paris 7th - <u>métro</u>: Invalides
Ph: 01.45.51.42.87 - Fax: 01.45.51.32.79
Lovely small patio inside.

10. Au Palais de Chaillot (28 rooms)
35 av. Raymond Poincaré, Paris 16th - <u>métro</u>: Trocadéro
Ph: 01.53.70.09.09 - Fax: 01.53.70.09.08
Only a few meters from the Eiffel tower.

The Top Ten Things to Know About French Restaurants

Paris is one of the world's greatest food capitals. Here are a few things you should know before going to a French restaurant.

1. **"Menu" versus "à la carte"**
   Restaurants generally serve a three-course meal at lunch and dinner. This fixed-price meal is called the "menu". If you don't choose this formula, you take "à la carte". It is always much cheaper to take the fixed-price "menu".

2. **Wines**
   "Cru" suggests a wine of superior quality. A "grand cru" or "premier cru" should be even more superior wine. Wine in "carafe" or "pichet" is usually ordinary table wine.

3. **Water**
   A "carafe d'eau" means tap water while "eau minérale" means a bottle of mineral water, "gazeuse" for carbonated or "plate" for not.

4. **Service and tax included ("service compris")**
   The prices that figure on the menu include service and tax.

5. **Tipping**
   Although the service is already included in the price, you can leave a tip for a very friendly waiter.

6. **Lunch and dinner time**
   Lunch is served between noon and 2 pm or 2.30 pm. Dinner is served between 7 pm and 10 pm or 11 pm. Some restaurants serve all night.

7. **Fromage ou Dessert**
   After the main course, you can choose cheese or dessert, or both. Most fixed-price menus include "cheese or dessert" or "cheese and dessert".

8. **Espresso**
   Another very French habit: take an espresso at the end of the meal. Be aware that if you ask for a "coffee", you won't get a large cup of coffee, but a small espresso!

9. Bistrot versus Brasserie

Bistrots and Brasseries are both very Parisian institutions. The bistrot is a kind of wine bar which serves simple and traditional home-style cooking. The brasserie is the French version of the pubs: single course dishes served with a beer.

10. Smoking / Non-smoking

Although it is a legal requirement to have two separate rooms, smoking and non-smoking, you'll notice that many restaurants, especially the small bistrots and cafés, do not really respect the law.

The Top Ten Places to Eat (High End)

Paris has some of the finest restaurants in the world. Expect to spend more than 800F per person.

1. Lucas Carton
9 place de la Madeleine, Paris 8th - <u>métro</u>: Madeleine
Ph: 01.42.65.22.90
Very creative cuisine. Don't miss the famous Apicius duck!

2. L'Ambroisie
9 place des Vosges, Paris 4th - <u>métro</u>: Saint-Paul
Ph: 01.42.78.51.45
Very refined cooking, in a splendid Renaissance decor.

3. Alain Ducasse
59 av. R. Poincaré, Paris 16th - <u>métro</u>: Victor Hugo
Ph: 01.47.27.12.27
Classical French cuisine.

4. La Tour d'Argent
17 quai de Tournelle, Paris 5th - <u>métro</u>: Cardinal-Lemoine
Ph: 01.43.54.23.31
A very famous address with the best view of Notre-Dame.

5. Les Ambassadeurs (Hôtel de Crillon)
10 place de la Concorde, Paris 8th - <u>métro</u>: Concorde
Ph: 01.44.71.16.16

6. Cercle Ledoyen
Carré des Champs-Elysées, Paris 8th - <u>métro</u>: Concorde or Champs-Elysées
Ph: 01.53.05.10.00 - Fax: 01.47.42.55.01
Excellent Northern French cuisine with specialties cooked in beer.

7. Taillevent
15 rue Lamennais, Paris 8th - <u>métro</u>: Charles de Gaulle-Etoile
Ph: 01.44.95.15.01 - Fax: 01.42.25.95.18

8. Guy Savoy

18 rue Troyon, Paris 17th - <u>métro</u>: Charles de Gaulle-Etoile
Ph: 01.43.80.40.61
Don't miss the delicious Mille-Feuille.

9. Le Grand Véfour

17 rue de Beaujolais, Paris 1st - <u>métro</u>: Palais-Royal
Ph: 01.42.96.56.27 - Fax: 01.42.86.80.71
A somptuous restaurant under the arcades of the Palais-Royal.

10. L'Arpège

84 rue de Varenne, Paris 7th - <u>métro</u>: Varenne
Ph: 01.47.05.09.06 - Fax: 01.44.18.98.39
Great food with original dishes.

The Top Ten Places to Eat (High Priced)

Still "Grande cuisine", but more affordable than the famous addresses listed before. Expect to spend between 300F and 600F per person.

I. Le Relais Louis XIII
8 rue des Grands Augustins, Paris 6th - <u>métro</u>: St-Michel
Ph: 01.43.26.75.96
Managed by Manuel Martinez, former cooking chef at the Tour d'Argent. Excellent food at reasonable prices.

2. Jacques Cagna
14 rue des Grands Augustins, Paris 6th - <u>métro</u>: St-Michel
Ph: 01.43.26.49.39
Excellent food, beautiful setting.

3. Carré des Feuillants
14 rue de Castiglione, Paris 1st - <u>métro</u>: Tuileries
Ph: 01.42.86.82.82
A classic in Paris.

4. Le Violon d'Ingres
135 rue Saint-Dominique, Paris 7th - <u>métro</u>: Solférino
Ph: 01.45.55.15.05
Delicious dishes, cozy atmosphere.

5. Faugeron
52 rue de Longchamp, Paris 16th - <u>métro</u>: Victor Hugo
Ph: 01.47.04.24.53

6. Le Dôme
108 blvd du Montparnasse, Paris 14th - <u>métro</u>: Montparnasse
Ph: 01.43.35.25.81

7. Benoit
20 rue Saint-Martin, Paris 4th - <u>métro</u>: Hôtel-de-Ville
Ph: 01.42.72.25.76

8. Marius et Jeannette
4 av. George V, Paris 8th - <u>métro</u>: George V
Ph: 01.47.23.41.88

9. Le Petit Bedon

38 rue Pergolèse, Paris 16th - <u>métro</u>: Porte Maillot
Ph: 01.45.00.23.66 - Fax: 01.45.00.44.03

10. Le Relais du Parc

55 av. Raymond Poincaré, Paris 16th - <u>métro</u>: Victor Hugo
Ph: 01.44.05.66.10 - Fax: 01.44.05.66.00
*Run by Alain Ducasse, this restaurant offers an excellent
menu. Pleasant terrace in the summer.*

The Top Ten Places to Eat (Medium Priced)

Paris has many restaurants serving very good food at reasonable prices (between 150F and 300F per person).

I. Le Petit Zinc
11 rue St-Benoit, Paris 6th - <u>métro</u>: St-Germain-des-Prés
Ph: 01.42.61.20.60
Excellent cooking in a lovely decor.

2. Epi Dupin
11 rue Dupin, Paris 6th - <u>métro</u>: Sèvres-Babylone
Ph: 01.42.22.64.56
Creative cuisine with a Mediterranean touch. Not to be missed. Reservations essential.

3. L'Excuse
14 rue Charles V, Paris 4th - <u>métro</u>: Saint-Paul
Ph: 01.42.77.98.97 - Fax: 01.42.77.88.55
Very good fixed-price menu at 165F.

4. Le Procope
13 rue de l'Ancienne Comédie, Paris 6th - <u>métro</u>: Odéon
Ph: 01.40.46.79.00 - Fax: 01.40.46.79.09
Le Procope is the oldest café in the world (1686) and has been entirely renovated. La Fontaine, Voltaire, Daudet, Oscar Wilde and Verlaine regularly came here.

5. Coco et sa Maison
18 rue de Bayen, Paris 17th - <u>métro</u>: Place des Ternes
Ph: 01.45.74.73.73 - Fax: 01.45.74.73.52
Very welcoming with excellent cooking.

6. Bofinger
5-7 rue de Bastille, Paris 11th - <u>métro</u>: Bastille
Ph: 01.42.72.87.82
Very typical Parisian brasserie, with one of the most beautiful and authentic belle epoque decors.

7. Au Bourguignon du Marais

52 rue François Miron, Paris 4th - <u>métro</u>: Saint-Paul
Ph: 01.48.87.15.40
Excellent bistrot in the heart of the Marais.

8. Au Bon Accueil

14 rue de Montessuy, Paris 7th - <u>métro</u>: Pont de l'Alma
Ph: 01.47.05.46.11
Lively and friendly atmosphere in this simple bistrot which has become very popular. Don't miss the excellent "cuisine du marché".

9. Philippe Detourbe

8 rue Nicolas Charlet, Paris 15th - <u>métro</u>: Pasteur
Ph: 01.42.19.08.59
Delicious dishes at reasonable prices.

10. Casa Bini

36 rue Grégoire-de-Tours, Paris 6th - <u>métro</u>: Odéon
Ph: 01.46.34.07.32
Excellent Tuscan cuisine.

The Top Ten Places to Eat (Inexpensive)

You do not need to spend more than 150F for a delicious meal!

1. Chez Clément
   6 addresses in Paris, including:
   47 av. de Wagram, Paris 17th - <u>métro</u>: Ternes
   Ph: 01.53.81.97.00
   123 av des Champs-Elysées, Paris 8th - <u>métro</u>: George V
   Ph: 01.40.73.87.00
   Chain of casual restaurants decorated like welcoming and cozy homes. Serve good traditional French cuisine at very reasonable prices.

2. Restaurant des Beaux-Arts
   11 rue Bonaparte, Paris 6th - <u>métro</u>: St-Germain-des-Prés
   Ph: 01.43.26.92.64
   Simple and good home-style cooking.

3. Les Noces de Jeannette
   14 rue Favart, Paris 2nd - <u>métro</u>: Richelieu-Drouot
   Ph: 01.42.96.36.89
   Very welcoming bistrot, which has an excellent fixed-price menu.

4. Le Patio Provençal
   116 rue des Dames, Paris 17th - <u>métro</u>: Villiers
   Ph: 01.42.93.73.73
   Tasteful dishes from Provence.

5. Osteria del Passe-partout
   20 rue de l'Hirondelle, Paris 6th - <u>métro</u>: St-Michel
   Ph: 01.46.34.14.54
   Very good Italian cooking at reasonable prices.

6. Chez Marianne
   2 rue des Hospitalières-Saint-Gervais, Paris 4th - <u>métro</u>: Saint-Paul or Hôtel-de-ville
   Ph: 01.42.72.18.86
   Jewish specialties from Central Europe. Very nice terrace in Summer.

7. Dame tartine

2 rue Brisemiche, Paris 4th - <u>métro</u>: Hôtel-de-Ville or Les
Halles
Ph: 01.42.77.32.22
*Pleasant terrace over the fanciful and colorful fountains by
Jean Tinguely and Niki de Saint-Phalle.*

8. Lescure

7 rue de Mondovi, Paris 1st - <u>métro</u>: Concorde
Ph: 01.42.60.18.91
A bargain in this neighborhood!

9. Chartier

7 rue du Faubourg-Montmartre, Paris 9th - <u>métro</u>: Rue
Montmartre
Ph: 01.47.70.86.29
*Although the food is ordinary, people come here for the
atmosphere. Around 50 francs per person.*

10. Orestias

4 rue Grégoire-de-Tours, Paris 6th - <u>métro</u>: Odéon
Ph: 01.43.54.62.01
Greek and French food. Serves a 44F fixed-price menu.

The Top Ten Restaurants with a View

I. La Tour d'Argent
17 quai de Tournelle, Paris 5th - <u>métro</u>: Cardinal-Lemoine
Ph: 01.43.54.23.31
A very famous address with the best view of Notre-Dame.

2. Jules Verne
Tour Eiffel (second floor), Champ de Mars, Paris 7th - <u>métro</u>:
Trocadéro or Dupleix or RER Champ de Mars-Tour Eiffel
Ph: 01.45.55.61.44
For a romantic evening. Excellent cooking.

3. La Maison Blanche
15 av. Montaigne, Paris 8th - <u>métro</u>: Alma Marceau
Ph: 01.47.23.55.99 - Fax: 01.47.20.09.56
*From the rooftop of the Theâtre des Champs-Elysées, nice
view over the Seine and the capital.*

4. Ziriab
Institut de Monde Arabe (9th floor)
1 rue des Fossés St-Bernard, Paris 5th - <u>métro</u>: Jussieu
Ph: 01.46.33.47.70
Excellent Arabic food.

5. Ciel de Paris
Tour Montparnasse (56th floor)
33 av. du Maine, Paris 14th - <u>métro</u>: Montparnasse
Ph: 01.45.38.52.35

6. Altitude 95
Tour Eiffel (1st floor), Champ de Mars, Paris 7th - <u>métro</u>:
Trocadéro or Dupleix or RER Champ de Mars-Tour Eiffel
Ph: 01.45.55.20.04
Good address, less expensive than the Jules Verne restaurant.

7. Morot-Gaudry
6 rue de la Cavalerie, Paris 15th - <u>métro</u>: La Motte-Picquet
Ph: 01.46.33.47.70
Nice view of the Eiffel tower from the 6th floor of a building.

8. Toupary
Samaritaine (5th floor)
2 quai du Louvre, Paris 1st - <u>métro</u>: Pont-Neuf
Ph: 01.40.41.29.29

9. Patachou
9 place du Tertre, Paris 18th - <u>métro</u>: Anvers
Ph: 01.42.51.06.06
Pleasant terrace overlooking Paris.

10. Le Totem
Palais de Chaillot, 1 place du Trocadéro, Paris 16th - <u>métro</u>:
Trocadéro
Ph: 01.47.27.28.29 - Fax: 01.47.27.53.01

The Top Ten Restaurants with a Terrace

If you are in Paris between June and September, you will appreciate having lunch or dinner on a terrace, sometimes far from the noise of the city.

1. **Maison de l'Amérique Latine**
   217 blvd St-Germain, Paris 7th - <u>métro</u>: Solférino
   Ph: 01.45.49.33.23 - Fax: 01.40.49.03.94
   Candlelight dinner in an incredible decor: a huge park in the heart of St-Germain district. Reservations essential.

2. **La Cour d'Honneur - Le Patio**
   Hôtel Crillon
   10 place de la Concorde - <u>métro</u>: Concorde
   Ph: 01.44.71.16.16
   Great address for those who can afford it.

3. **Atalante**
   10 rue Chateaubriand, Paris 8th - <u>métro</u>: George V
   Ph: 01.45.63.23.05
   Pleasant garden.

4. **Le Chalet des Iles**
   Lac du Bois de Boulogne, Paris 16th - <u>métro</u>: Rue de la Pompe
   Ph: 01.42.88.04.69 - Fax: 01.45.25.41.57
   Nice address, far from the noises of the capital.

5. **Café des Lettres**
   53 rue de Verneuil, Paris 7th - <u>métro</u>: Rue-du-Bac
   Ph: 01.42.22.52.17

6. **Le Récamier**
   4 rue Récamier, Paris 7th - <u>métro</u>: Sèvres-Babylone
   Ph: 01.45.48.86.58

7. **Le Jardin des Cygnes**
   Hôtel Prince de Galles
   33 av. George-V, Paris 8th - <u>métro</u>: George V
   Ph: 01.47.23.55.11
   Chic address.

8. Fontanarosa

28 blvd de Garibaldi, Paris 15th - <u>métro</u>: Cambronne
Ph: 01.45.66.97.84
Specialties from the south of Italy.

9. Fond de Cour

3 rue Ste-Croix-de-la-Bretonnerie, Paris 4th - <u>métro</u>: St-Paul
or Hôtel-de-Ville
Ph: 01.42.74.71.52
Pleasant courtyard.

10. La Bûcherie

91 rue de la Bûcherie, Paris 5th - <u>métro</u>: Maubert-Mutualité
Ph: 01.43.29.73.57

The Top Ten "In" Restaurants

The places to see and be seen...

I. La Maison Blanche
15 av. Montaigne, Paris 8th - <u>métro</u>: Alma Marceau
Ph: 01.47.23.55.99 - Fax: 01.47.20.09.56
Very chic.

2. Buddha Bar
8 rue Boissy d'Anglas, Paris 8th - <u>métro</u>: Concorde
Ph: 01.53.03.90.00
A "hot" place full of slick trendies. American-Oriental cuisine.

3. La Plage
Port de Javel, Paris 15th - <u>métro</u>: Javel
Ph: 01.40.59.41.00 - Fax: 01.40.59.81.50
Nice atmosphere along the Seine.

4. Bermuda Onion
16 rue Linois, Paris 15th - <u>métro</u>: Charles Michel
Ph: 01.45.75.11.11
Trendy address, good food, warm atmosphere and very sexy waitresses!

5. Café Marly
93 rue de Rivoli, Paris 1st - <u>métro</u>: Palais Royal
Ph: 01.49.26.06.60
A great view on the Pyramide du Louvre. Very cozy inside.

6. L'Appart
9 rue du Colisée, Paris 8th - <u>métro</u>: George V
Ph: 01.53.75.16.34 - Fax: 01.53.76.15.39
Decorated like a private home, with a living room, a dining room, a library ...

7. Restaurant de l'Hôtel Costes
239 rue Saint-Honoré, Paris 1st - <u>métro</u>: Concorde
Ph: 01.42.44.50.26

8. Montecristo Café
68 av des Champs-Elysées, Paris 8th - <u>métro</u>: Franklin D. Roosevelt
Ph: 01.45.62.30.86 - Fax: 01.45.62.22.76
A Cuban café, restaurant, bar and nightclub.

9. Le Barfly
49 av. George V, Paris 8th - <u>métro</u>: George V
Ph: 01.53.67.8460

10. Opium Café
5 rue Elzevir, Paris 3rd - <u>métro</u>: Saint-Paul
Ph: 01.40.29.93.40

The Top Ten Foreign Food Restaurants

If you have enough of French food, here are some good alternatives:

I. Noura
27-29 av. Marceau, Paris 16th - <u>métro</u>: Alma-Marceau
Ph: 01.47.23.20.20 - Fax: 01.49.52.01.26
Or 121 blvd du Montparnasse - <u>métro</u>: Vavin
Ph: 01.43.20.19.19
Paris' best Lebanese restaurant.

2. Au Coco de Mer
34 blvd St-Marcel, Paris 5th - <u>métro</u>: St-Marcel
Ph: 01.47.07.06.64
Excellent cooking from the Seychelles.

3. Flora Danica - La Maison du Danemark
142 av des Champs-Elysées Paris 8th - <u>métro</u>: Charles de Gaulle-Etoile
Ph: 01.44.13.86.26
A chic and trendy address to savor specialties from Denmark in a charming patio.

4. La Famiglia
2 rue Waldeck-Rousseau, Paris 17th - <u>métro</u>: Porte Maillot
Ph: 01.45.74.20.28
Paris' best pasta.

5. Isami
4 quai d'Orléans, Paris 4th - <u>métro</u>: Pont-Marie
Ph: 01.40.46.06.97
An excellent Japanese restaurant in the heart of Ile St-Louis.

6. El Picaflor
9 rue Lacépède, Paris 5th - <u>métro</u>: Place Monge
Ph: 01.43.31.06.01
Paris's best Peruvian restaurant.

7. Mavrommatis - Le restaurant
42 rue Daubenton, Paris 5th - <u>métro</u>: Censier-Daubenton
Ph: 01.43.31.17.17
Excellent Greek food (moussaka, mezze...)

8. El Sereno

8 rue Boutebrie, Paris 5th - <u>métro</u>:
Ph: 01.46.33.86.24
If you like paellas, tapas, and flamenco, don't miss it!

9. L'Atlas

10-12 blvd St-Germain, Paris 5th - <u>métro</u>: Maubert-Mutualité
Ph: 01.46.33.86.98
Delicious specialties from Morocco (couscous, tagines...).

10. Taski Delesk

4 rue des Fossés St-Jacques, Paris 5th - RER Luxembourg
Ph: 01.43.26.55.55
Favorful specialties from Tibet.

The Top Ten Restaurants in the 4th Arrondissement (Marais)

1. L'Ambroisie
9 place des Vosges, Paris 4th - <u>métro</u>: Saint-Paul
Ph: 01.42.78.51.45
Decor, food, service, location: everything is perfect!

2. L'Excuse
14 rue Charles V, Paris 4th - <u>métro</u>: Saint-Paul
Ph: 01.42.77.98.97 - Fax: 01.42.77.88.55
Excellent fixed-price menu at 165F. Very good service.

3. L'Enoteca
25 rue Charles V, Paris 4th - <u>métro</u>: Saint-Paul
Ph: 01.42.78.91.44
Excellent Italian food in elegant atmosphere typical of the Marais.

4. Chez Marianne
2 rue des Hospitalières-Saint-Gervais, Paris 4th - <u>métro</u>: Saint-Paul or Hôtel-de-Ville
Ph: 01.42.72.18.86
Jewish specialties from Central Europe. Very nice terrace in Summer.

5. La Guirlande de Julie
25 place des Vosges, Paris 4th - <u>métro</u>: Saint-Paul or Chemin-Vert
Ph: 01.48.87.94.07
In the summer it's very romantic to have dinner under the arcades of Paris' most elegant square.

6. Jo Goldenberg
7 rue des Rosiers, Paris 4th - <u>métro</u>: Saint-Paul
Ph: 01.48.87.20.16
Paris' most famous Jewish restaurant.

7. Le Gamin de Paris
49 rue Vieille du Temple, Paris 4th - <u>métro</u>: Saint-Paul
Ph: 01.42.78.97.24
A favorite of the Parisians.

8. Au Bourguignon du Marais

52 rue François Miron, Paris 4th - <u>métro</u>: Saint-Paul
Ph: 01.48.87.15.40
Excellent bistro in the heart of the Marais.

9. Le Rouge-Gorge

8 rue Saint-Paul, Paris 4th - <u>métro</u>: Saint-Paul
Ph: 01.48.04.75.89
Very good food in a rustic decor.

10. Le Coude Fou

12 rue du Bourg-Tibourg, Paris 4th - <u>métro</u>: Hôtel-de-Ville or
Saint-Paul
Ph: 01.42.77.15.16

The Top Ten Restaurants in the 6th Arrondissement (Odéon, St-Germain-des-Prés)

I. **Le Relais Louis XIII**
8 rue des Grands Augustins, Paris 6th - <u>métro</u>: St-Michel
Ph: 01.43.26.75.96
Managed by Manuel Martinez, former cooking chef at the Tour d'Argent. Excellent food.

2. **Le Bouillon Racine**
3 rue Racine, Paris 6th - <u>métro</u>: Cluny la Sorbonne or Odéon
Ph: 01.44.32.15.60
Excellent cooking and charming atmosphere.

3. **Le Petit Zinc**
11 rue St-Benoit, Paris 6th - <u>métro</u>: St-Germain-des-Prés
Ph: 01.42.61.20.60
Refined cuisine in a beautiful decor.

4. **L'o à la bouche**
157 blvd du Montparnasse, Paris 6th - <u>métro</u>: Vavin or RER Port Royal
Ph: 01.43.26.26.53
Great fixed-price menu at 150F.

5. **Chez Dumonet**
117 rue du Cherche-Midi, Paris 6th - <u>métro</u>: Rennes
Ph: 01.45.48.52.40
Very welcoming bistrot with specialties from the southwest of France.

6. **Bistrot de la Grille**
14 rue Mabillon, Paris 6th - <u>métro</u>: Mabillon
Ph: 01.43.54.16.87
Excellent dishes from Lyon.

7. **Osteria del Passe-partout**
20 rue de l'Hirondelle, Paris 6th - <u>métro</u>: St-Michel
Ph: 01.46.34.14.54
Very good Italian cooking at reasonable prices.

8. La Cafetière
21 rue Mazarine, Paris 6th - <u>métro</u>: Odéon
Ph: 01.46.33.76.90
Good Italian specialties.

9. La Méditerranée
2 place de l'Odéon, Paris 6th - <u>métro</u>: Odéon
Ph: 01.43.26.02.30

10. Bistrot Mazarine
42 rue Mazarine, Paris 6th - <u>métro</u>: Odéon or Mabillon
Ph: 01.43.29.99.01
Very good pasta.

The Top Ten Restaurants in the 8th Arrondissement (Champs-Elysées)

1. **Taillevent**
   15 rue Lamennais, Paris 8th - <u>métro</u>: Charles de Gaulle-Etoile
   Ph: 01.44.95.15.01 - Fax: 01.42.25.95.18
   A must in Paris if you can afford it.

2. **Guy Savoy**
   18 rue Troyon, Paris 17th - <u>métro</u>: Charles de Gaulle-Etoile
   Ph: 01.43.80.40.61
   Another "grande cuisine" address, very pricey.

3. **Buddha Bar**
   8 rue Boissy d'Anglas, Paris 8th - <u>métro</u>: Concorde
   Ph: 01.53.03.90.00
   A very trendy place. American-Oriental cuisine.

4. **Le Fouquet's**
   99 av des Champs-Elysées Paris 8th - <u>métro</u>: George-V
   Ph: 01.47.23.70.60
   Very famous address on Champs-Elysées. Orson Welles' favorite café.

5. **Le Jardin des Cygnes**
   Hôtel Prince de Galles
   33 av. George V, Paris 8th - <u>métro</u>: George V
   Ph: 01.47.23.55.11
   Nice terrace in the summer.

6. **Le Boeuf sur le Toit**
   34 rue du Colisée, Paris 8th - <u>métro</u>: Franklin Roosevelt
   Ph: 01.43.59.83.80
   Excellent seafood.

7. **La Fermette Marbeuf 1900**
   5 rue Marbeuf, Paris 8th - <u>métro</u>: Franklin Roosevelt
   Ph: 01.53.23.08.00 - Fax: 01.53.23.08.09
   Worth it for the room which is listed among the historical monuments.

8. Chez Clément

123 av des Champs-Elysées, Paris 8th - <u>métro</u>: George V
Ph: 01.40.73.87.00
Serves good traditional French cuisine at very reasonable prices.

9. Plaza Berri

4 rue de Berri, Paris 8th - <u>métro</u>: Franklin Roosevelt
Ph: 01.43.59.46.20
Good and inexpensive pizza and pasta.

10. Planet Hollywood

78 av des Champs-Elysées, Paris 8th - <u>métro</u>: George V
Ph: 01.53.83.78.27
For Americans who miss their home... good salads and good Tex-Mex food.

The Top Ten Wine Bars (Bars à Vin, Bistrots)

Friendly places where you can taste wine and accompany your glass with cold or hot dishes. Some of them look more like restaurants and are often called "bistrots".

I. L'Ange Vin
168 rue Montmartre, Paris 2nd - <u>métro</u>: Rue Montmartre
Ph: 01.42.36.20.20
Typical Parisian decor. A great choice of wines.

2. Jacques Mélac
42 rue Léon Frot, Paris 11th - <u>métro</u>: Charonne
Ph: 01.43.70.59.27 - Fax: 01.43.70.73.10
Produces its own wine! Always crowded.

3. Le Rubis
10 rue du Marché-Saint-Honoré, Paris 1st - <u>métro</u>: Tuileries
Ph: 01.42.61.03.34
After work many people come here and drink a glass of wine while leaning on barrels on the sidewalk. Guaranteed exciting atmosphere during the "Beaujolais nouveau" event.

4. Les Bacchantes
21 rue Caumartin, Paris 9th - <u>métro</u>: La Madeleine or Havre-Caumartin
Ph: 01.42.65.25.35 - Fax: 01.47.42.65.87

5. Le Relais Chablisien
4 rue Bertin-Poirée, Paris 1st - <u>métro</u>: Châtelet or Pont-Neuf
Ph: 01.45.08.53.73

6. Phénix Café
4 rue du Faubourg-Poissonnière, Paris 10th - <u>métro</u>: Bonne-Nouvelle
Ph: 01.47.70.35.40

7. Le Rouge-Gorge
8 rue Saint-Paul, Paris 4th - <u>métro</u>: Saint-Paul
Ph: 01.48.04.75.89
Very good food in a rustic decor.

8. Le Petit Fer à Cheval
30 rue Vieille-du-Temple, Paris 4th - <u>métro</u>: Saint-Paul or
Hôtel-de-ville
Ph: 01.42.72.47.47

9. Le Coude Fou
12 rue du Bourg-Tibourg, Paris 4th - <u>métro</u>: Hôtel-de-Ville or
Saint-Paul
Ph: 01.42.77.15.16

10. La Tour de Pierre
53 rue Dauphine, Paris 6th - <u>métro</u>: Odéon
Ph: 01.43.26.08.93

The Top Ten Tea Rooms (Salons de Thé)

The "salons de thé" are cozy places that serve delicious quiches, salads and pastries for lunch or afternoon tea.

1. A Priori Thé
35 galerie Vivienne, Paris 2nd - <u>métro</u>: Palais-Royal or Bourse
Ph: 01.42.97.48.75 - Fax: 01.42.97.46.31
Delicious food in a lovely place.

2. Le Loir dans la Théierè
3 rue des Rosiers, Paris 4th - <u>métro</u>: Saint-Paul
Ph: 01.42.72.90.61
Very charming.

3. Ladurée
16 rue Royale, Paris 8th - <u>métro</u>: Concorde
Ph: 01.42.60.21.79
Ideal after shopping.

4. Le Café Maure de la Mosquée de Paris
39 rue Geoffroy-St-Hilaire, Paris 5th - <u>métro</u>: Jussieu
Ph: 01.43.31.18.14
An absolute haven! Try the North African and Middle Eastern pastries with a sweet mint tea or a Turkish coffee.

5. Mariage Frères
30 rue du Bourg-Tibourg, Paris 4th - <u>métro</u>: Saint-Paul or Hôtel-de-ville
Ph: 01.42.72.28.11
The best tea in Paris.

6. Les Enfants gâtés
43 rue des Francs-Bourgeois, Paris 4th - <u>métro</u>: Saint-Paul
Ph: 01.42.77.07.63

7. Angelina
226 rue de Rivoli, Pars 1st - <u>métro</u>: Concorde or Tuileries
Ph: 01.42.60.82.00
Try their very thick hot chocolate.

8. La Charlotte de l'Isle
24 rue Saint-Louis-en-l'Ile, Paris 4th - <u>métro</u>: Pont-Marie or
Sully-Morland
Ph: 01.43.54.25.83

9. The Tea Caddy
14 rue St Julien le Pauvre, Paris 5th - <u>métro</u>: Maubert-
Mutualité
Ph: 01.43.54.15.56

10. L'Ebouillanté
6 rue des Barres, Paris 4th - <u>métro</u>: Pont-Marie or Hôtel-de-
Ville
Ph: 01.42.71.09.69
The tiniest salon de thé.

The Top Ten Brunches

While the brunch has not been part of the French people's dining habits, today more and more restaurants or "salons de thé" serve a brunch during the weekend or just on Sundays.

I. **Le Jardin des Cygnes**
   33 av. George-V, Paris 8th - <u>métro</u>: George V
   Ph: 01.47.23.55.11
   Excellent brunch on Sundays, though pricey.

2. **A Priori Thé**
   35 galerie Vivienne, Paris 2nd - <u>métro</u>: Palais-Royal or Bourse
   Ph: 01.42.97.48.75 - Fax: 01.42.97.46.31
   Delicious brunch on Saturdays and Sundays.

3. **Le Loir dans la Théiere**
   3 rue des Rosiers, Paris 4th - <u>métro</u>: Saint-Paul
   Ph: 01.42.72.90.61
   Brunch on Saturdays and Sundays.

4. **Les Fous de l'Ile**
   33 rue des Deux-Ponts, Paris 4th - <u>métro</u>: Pont-Marie
   Ph: 01.43.25.76.67
   Brunch on Sundays.

5. **The Studio**
   41 rue du Temple, Paris 4th - <u>métro</u>: Hôtel-de-Ville
   Ph: 01.42.74.10.38
   Tex-Mex brunch on Saturdays and Sundays.

6. **L'Appart**
   9 rue du Colisée, Paris 8th - <u>métro</u>: George V
   Ph: 01.53.75.16.34 - Fax: 01.53.76.15.39
   Decorated like a private home, with a living room, a dining room, a library...

7. **La Fourmi Ailée**
   8 rue du Fouarre, Paris 5th - <u>métro</u>: Saint-Michel or Maubert-Mutualité
   Ph: 01.43.29.40.99
   Very charming. Brunch on Saturdays and Sundays.

8. Tea Follies

6 pl. Gustave-Toudouze, Paris 9th - <u>métro</u>: St-Georges
Ph: 01.42.80.08.44

9. Les Etages

35 rue Vieille-du-Temple, Paris 4th - <u>métro</u>: Saint-Paul or
Hôtel-de-ville
Ph: 01.42.79.72.00
Brunch on Sundays.

10. Web Bar

32 rue de Picardie, Paris 3rd - <u>métro</u>: Temple
Ph: 01.42.72.66.55 - Fax: 01.42.72.66.75 - Internet http://
www.webbar.fr
The best cybercafé in Paris.

The Top Ten Cafés

You'll find a café on every corner in Paris. They all have in common: sidewalk tables, hurried waiters, and Parisians drinking espresso and smoking cigarettes. The most famous cafés are those in the 6th arrondissement where intellectuals and artists have always met.

1. **Café de Flore**
   173 blvd St-Germain, Paris 6th - <u>métro</u>: St-Germain-des-Prés
   Ph: 01.45.48.55.25
   Picasso, Jean-Paul Sartre, Simone de Beauvoir and many other intellectuals frequented this café.

2. **Les Deux Magots**
   6 place St-Germain-des-Prés, Paris 6th - <u>métro</u>: St-Germain-des-Prés
   Ph: 01.45.48.55.25
   Another literary café frequented by intellectuals.

3. **La Coupole**
   102 blvd Montparnasse, Paris 14th - <u>métro</u>: Montparnasse or Vavin
   Ph: 01.43.20.14.20
   Hemingway, Aragon, Colette, Simone de Beauvoir and others wrote some of their greatest works here.

4. **Café Marly**
   93 rue de Rivoli, Paris 1st - <u>métro</u>: Palais Royal
   Ph: 01.49.26.06.60
   A great view on the Pyramide du Louvre. Cozy atmosphere inside.

5. **La Closerie des Lilas**
   171 blvd du Montparnasse, Paris 6th - <u>métro</u>: Port-Royal
   Ph: 01.43.54.21.68
   The home of several generations of intellectuals, from Verlaine, Baudelaire, and Malarmé to Max Jacob, Lenin and Hemingway.

6. **Café de la Paix**
   12 blvd des Capucines, Paris 9th - <u>métro</u>: Opéra
   Ph: 01.40.07.30.20

7. Le Fouquet's

99 av des Champs-Elysées, Paris 8th - <u>métro</u>: George V
Ph: 01.47.23.70.60
Very famous address on the Champs-Elysées. A favorite of Orson Welles.

8. La Palette

43 rue de Seine, Paris 6th - <u>métro</u>: Mabillon
Ph: 01.43.26.68.15
The favorite of students in the heart of the Quartier Latin.

9. Brasserie Lipp

151 blvd Saint-Germain, Paris 6th - <u>métro</u>: St-Germain-des-Prés
Ph: 01.45.48.53.91
Open in 1880, it was always the rendez-vous for artists and politicians. Hemingway wrote 'Farewell to Arms' there.

10. Café du Dôme

108 blvd Montparnasse, Paris 14th - <u>métro</u>: Vavin
Ph: 01.43.35.25.81

The Top Ten Cybercafés

In the last few years many "cybercafés" opened in Paris. A cybercafé is a new phenomenon that lets you surf on the Internet while drinking a glass of wine.

I. Web Bar

32 rue de Picardie, Paris 3rd - <u>métro</u>: Temple
Ph: 01.42.72.66.55 - Fax: 01.42.72.66.75
E-mail: webbar@webbar.fr
Web Site URL: http://www.webbar.fr
The best cybercafé in Paris: beautiful decor, trendy and cheap. Not to be missed!

2. Café Orbital Quartier Latin

13 rue de Médicis, Paris 6th - <u>métro</u>: Odéon
Ph: 01.43.25.76.77
Web Site URL: http://orbital.fr

3. Cyberia

Centre Georges Pompidou, Paris 4th - <u>métro</u>: Les Halles
Ph: 01.44.54.53.49
Web Site URL: http://www.cyberia.fr

4. Planet Cyber Café

173 rue de Vaugirard, Paris 15th - <u>métro</u>: Pasteur
Ph: 01.45.67.71.14
Web Site URL: http://www.starnet.fr/planet-cybercafé

5. Virgin Mégastore

52 av. des Champs-Elysées, Paris 8th - <u>métro</u>: George V
Ph: 01.49.53.50.00
Web Site URL: http://www.virgin.fr

6. Cyberport

Forum des Halles, Paris 1st - <u>métro</u>: Les Halles
Ph: 01.44.76.62.00
Web Site URL: http://www.vdp.fr

7. High Tech Café

66 Blvd Montparnasse, Paris 14th - <u>métro</u>: Montparnasse
Ph: 01.45.38.67.61
Web Site URL: http://www.htc.fr

8. Bistro Internet

Galeries Lafayette, Paris 9th - <u>métro</u>: Auber, Opéra, or Chaussée d'Antin
Ph: 01.42.82.30.33
Web Site URL: http://www.bistrointernet.fr

9. Bonjour Tout le Monde

15 rue Pérignon, Paris 7th - <u>métro</u>: Ségur
Ph: 01.45.66.65.35
Web Site URL: http://www.micronet.fr/~roulez

10. Travel Café

2 rue d'Alleray, Paris 15th - <u>métro</u>: Vaugirard
Ph: 01.42.50.11.10
Web Site URL: http://www.abcvoyage.com

The Top Ten Gourmet and Specialty Food Shops

Here are the favorite addresses of Parisian gourmets.

1. **Berthillon**
   31 rue Saint-Louis-en-l'Ile, Paris 4th - <u>métro</u>: Pont-Marie
   Ph: 01.43.54.31.61
   The best ice cream in Paris.

2. **Fauchon**
   26 place de la Madeleine, Paris 8th - <u>métro</u>: Madeleine
   Ph: 01.47.42.60.11
   Luxury delicatessen.

3. **Hédiard**
   21 place de la Madeleine, Paris 8th - <u>métro</u>: Madeleine
   Ph: 01.43.12.88.77
   Luxury delicatessen. A large variety of spices.

4. **Flo Prestige**
   Among several addresses:
   42 place du Marché-St-Honoré, Paris 1st - <u>métro</u>: Pyramides
   Ph: 01.42.61.45.46
   36 av La Motte Picquet, Paris 7th - <u>métro</u>: Ecole Militaire
   Ph: 01.45.55.71.25
   10 rue St-Antoine, Paris 4th - <u>métro</u>: Bastille
   Ph: 01.53.01.9191
   Famous caterer at reasonable prices. Open very late.

5. **La Grande Epicerie**
   38 rue de Sèvres, Paris 7th - <u>métro</u>: Sèvre-Babylone
   Ph: 01.44.39.81.00

6. **Debauve & Gallais**
   30 rue des Saints-Pères, Paris 6th - <u>métro</u>: St-Germain-des-Prés
   Ph: 01.45.48.54.67
   Also 107, rue Jouffroy d'Abbans, 17th (<u>métro</u>: Charles de Gaulle-Etoile) and 33, rue de Vivienne, 2nd (<u>métro</u>: Bourse)
   Heaven on earth for chocolate lovers!

7. Lenôtre

48 av. Victor Hugo, Paris 16th - <u>métro</u>: Victor Hugo
Ph: 01.42.01.71.71
Famous French caterer Gaston Lenôtre has several boutiques in Paris.

8. Au Verger de la Madeleine

4 blvd Malesherbes, Paris 8th - <u>métro</u>: Madeleine
Ph: 01.42.65.51.99
Vintage wine merchant with an outstanding selection of wines and spirits.

9. Dalloyau

99-101 rue du Faubourg-S-Honoré, Paris 8th - <u>métro</u>: St-Philippe-du-Roule
Ph: 01.42.99.90.00
Very good pastries.

10. Poilâne

8 rue du Cherche-Midi, Paris 6th - <u>métro</u>: St-Sulpice
Ph: 01.45.48.42.59
Lionel Poilâne makes the most famous bread in the world.

The Top Ten Open-air Food Markets

Go off the beaten path and experience one of the numerous open-air food markets in Paris.

1. Rue Mouffetard
Paris 5th - <u>métro</u>: Censier-Daubenton
Very lively and picturesque place.

2. Rue Montorgueil
Paris 2nd - <u>métro</u>: Les Halles
Very lively street with old food shops.

3. Place d'Alligre,
Paris 12th - <u>métro</u>: Ledru-Rollin
The cheapest and most lively market in Paris.

4. Place Monge
Paris 5th - <u>métro</u>: Place Monge

5. Rue de Lévis
Paris 17th - <u>métro</u>: Villiers
Pleasant pedestrian street with a picturesque market.

6. Boulevard Richard-Lenoir
Paris 11th - <u>métro</u>: Bastille or Richard-Lenoir

7. Rue de Busi and Rue de Seine
Paris 6th - <u>métro</u>: Odéon

8. Rue Cler
Paris 7th - <u>métro</u>: Ecole Militaire

9. Rue de Passy
Paris 16th - <u>métro</u>: Passy

10. Avenue de Saxe
Paris 7th - <u>métro</u>: Duroc

The Top Ten Food Specialties

French cooking may be very different from a region to another. Here are the most typical French dishes, that you will eat nowhere else.

I. Blanquette de Veau
Veal cooked in white sauce, served with rice.

2. Boeuf Bourguignon
Beef cooked in red wine (from Burgundy).

3. Cassoulet
Sausage and chicken with beans (from Toulouse).

4. Foie gras
Very fine appetizer made of pure duck or goose liver (from the Southwest of France).

5. Coq au vin
Chicken in red wine.

6. Pot au feu
Beef and vegetable hotpot.

7. Choucroute
Variety of sausages served with sauerkraut (from Alsace).

8. Cuisses de grenouille
Frogs legs cooked with garlic, parsley, and butter.

9. Bouillabaisse
Marseille specialty consisting of a variety of fishes cooked together.

10. Escargots
Snails cooked with parsley and butter.

The Top Ten French Red Wines

French red wines are produced in different regions, of which the most famous are: Bordeaux (in the Southwest), Bourgogne (Burgundy), Loire valley, and Rhône valley.

1. **Médoc 1er cru** (Bordeaux)

2. **Vosne Romanée** (Bourgogne - Côtes de Nuits)

3. **Pomerol** (Bordeaux)

4. **Pommard** (Bourgogne - Côtes de Beaune)

5. **Saint Emilion** (Bordeaux)

6. **Saint Julien** (Bordeaux)

7. **Châteauneuf du Pape** (Côtes du Rhône)

8. **Aloxe Corton** (Bourgogne - Côtes de Beaune)

9. **Nuits Saint Georges** (Bourgogne - Côtes de Nuits)

10. **Saint-Joseph** (Côtes du Rhône)

The Top Ten French White Wines

Like red wines, white wines are produced in different regions.

1. **Sauterne** (Bordeaux)

2. **Pouilly-Fuissé** (Bourgogne)

3. **Condrieu** (Côtes du Rhône)

4. **Gewurtzraminer** (Alsace)

5. **Sancerre Blanc** (Loire)

6. **Pouilly-Fumé** (Loire Valley)

7. **Jurançon** (Southwest of France)

8. **Château Chalon** (Jura)

9. **Riesling** (Alsace)

10. **Graves Blanc** (Bordeaux)

The Top Ten French Champagnes

Most champagnes are produced in Reims area, at about 150km east of Paris.

1. **Dom Pérignon**

2. **Deutz**

3. **Moët & Chandon**

4. **Roderer**

5. **Ruinart**

6. **Veuve Cliquot**

7. **Mum**

8. **Taittinger**

9. **Piper-Heidsieck**

10. **Lanson**

The Top Ten French Beers

Although France is not the best place for beer, French beer is drunk in large quantities in the country.

1. **Kronembourg**

2. **Kanterbrau**

3. **Stella Artois**

4. **1664**

5. **Jeanlain**

6. **Pelforth**

7. **Jupiler**

8. **Killian's**

9. **Adelscott**

10. **La Bière du Démon**

The Top Ten Department Stores and Malls

Paris has great department stores, very representative of the Parisian chic.

1. Au Bon Marché
   22 rue de Sèvres, Paris 7th - <u>métro</u>: Sèvres-Babylone
   Ph: 01.44.39.80.00
   The most chic department store in Paris.

2. Galeries Lafayette-Haussmann
   40 blvd Haussmann, Paris 9th - <u>métro</u>: Chaussée d'Antin or Opéra
   Ph: 01.42.82.34.56
   A large department store with an outstanding perfume department.

3. Au Printemps Haussmann
   64 blvd Haussmann, Paris 9th - <u>métro</u>: Havre-Caumartin
   Ph: 01.42.82.57.87
   A large department store in an 1865 building classified as a national monument. Great view from the terrace on the roof.

4. La Samaritaine
   19 rue de la Monnaie, Paris 1st - <u>métro</u>: Pont-Neuf
   Ph: 01.40.41.20.20

5. Les Trois Quartiers
   23 blvd de la Madeleine, Paris 1st - <u>métro</u>: Madeleine
   Ph: 01.42.97.80.12
   An elegant shopping mall for men's and women's fashion (Kenzo, Yves Saint Laurent), as well as for gifts and home decoration. A sports store, Decathlon, just opened in December 1997.

6. Le Carroussel du Louvre
   Entrances on rue de Rivoli, through the Louvre museum or directly from the metro: - <u>métro</u>: Palais-Royal
   Open daily until 10 pm. Closed on Tuesdays.
   Small but beautiful shopping mall next to the Louvre museum, including a large Food Court.

7. Le Marché Saint-Germain

Entrance on rue Clément, Paris 6th - <u>métro</u>: Mabillon
Ph: 01.43.26.01.44
New shopping mall with 21 boutiques including ready-to-wear, shoes, accessories, beauty products.

8. Le Passage du Havre

14 rue du Havre, Paris 9th - <u>métro</u>: St-Lazare
A brand new place with 30 shops, including the FNAC (books, CDs, video...), Sephora (perfume and makeup) and Gap.

9. Franck et Fils

80 rue de Passy, Paris 16th - <u>métro</u>: Passy
Ph: 01.44.14.38.00
An upscale department store.

10. Les Quatre Temps

Esplanade de la Défense - <u>métro</u>: Grande Arche de la Défense
Large shopping complex with 250 boutiques. Also Marks & Spencer and Toys'R Us.

The Top Ten Chic Streets to Shop

Most Parisian stylish boutiques are concentrated in the 8th and 6th arrondissements.

1. Avenue Montaigne (Paris 8th)
Along the avenue Montaigne you'll find all the Haute Couture houses: Christian Dior, Christian Lacroix, Celine, Guy Laroche, Thierry Mugler.

2. Rue du Faubourg St Honoré (Paris 8th)
The other chic place in Paris, where you'll find, among others, Hermès, Guy Laroche, Versace, Yves Saint-Laurent, Lanvin, Karl Lagerfeld, Gucci, and Courrèges.

3. Boulevard Saint-Germain (Paris 6th)
The St-Germain-des-Prés is both chic and trendy. You'll see Sonia Rykiel, Daniel Hechter, Emporio Armani, Gérard Darel, Façonnable, and many others.

4. Rue Cambon (Paris 1st)
Chanel, Céline.

5. Rue Royale (Paris 8th)
Fashion (Cerruti 1881, Et Vous, Gérard Darel, Ralph Lauren) and tableware (Lalique, Christofle, Cristallerie Saint-Louis, Bernardaud).

6. Rue du Four (Paris 6th)
Max Mara, Irene Van Ryb.

7. Place Vendôme and Rue de la Paix (Paris 1st)
Cartier, Chanel, Van Cleef & Arpels, Boucheron, Chaumet.

8. Place des Victoires (Paris 2nd)
Kenzo, Cacharel.

9. Rue Saint-Honoré (Paris 1st)
Max Mara, Longchamp, Didier Lamarthe, Episode, Laurel.

10. Rue des Francs-Bourgeois (Paris 4th)
Trendy boutiques. One of the rare places where all shops are open on Sundays.

The Top Ten Haute Couture Houses

For many people, Paris means Haute Couture. Walk along the avenue Montaigne and you'll understand why.

I. Chanel
31 rue Cambon, Paris 1st - <u>métro</u>: Concorde
Ph: 01.42.86.28.00

2 Christian Dior
30 av. Montaigne, Paris 8th - <u>métro</u>: Franklin D. Roosevelt
Ph: 01.40.73.54.44

3. Yves Saint Laurent
5 av. Marceau, Paris 8th - <u>métro</u>: Alma-Marceau
Ph: 01.44.31.64.00 - Fax: 01.47.23.69.73

4. Christian Lacroix
73 rue du Faubourg St-Honoré, Paris 8th - <u>métro</u>: Miromesnil
Ph: 01.42.68.79.00 - Fax: 01.49.24.99.41

5. Emmanuel Ungaro
2 av. Montaigne, Paris 8th - <u>métro</u>: Alma-Marceau
Ph: 01.53.57.00.00

6. Givenchy
3 av. George V, Paris 8th - <u>métro</u>: Alma-Marceau
Ph: 01.44.31.50.00 - Fax: 01.47.20.44.96

7. Nina Ricci
39 av. Montaigne, Paris 8th - <u>métro</u>: Franklin D. Roosevelt
Ph: 01.49.52.56.00

8. Louis Féraud
88 rue du Faubourg St-Honoré, Paris 8th - <u>métro</u>: Champs-Elysées-Clémenceau
Ph: 01.42.65.27.29

9. Paco Rabanne
7 rue du Cherche Midi, Paris 6th - <u>métro</u>: St-Sulpice
Ph: 01.40.49.08.53

10. Jean-Louis Sherrer
51 av. Montaigne, Paris 8th - <u>métro</u>: Franklin D. Roosevelt
Ph: 01.42.99.05.79

The Top Ten Women's Wear

I. Max Mara
265 rue St-Honoré, Paris 1st - <u>métro</u>: Tuileries
Ph: 01.40.20.04.58
or 37 rue du Four, Paris 6th - <u>métro</u>: Mabillon
Ph: 01.43.29.91.10

2. Agnès B
13 rue Michelet, Paris 6th - RER Port Royal or <u>métro</u>: Vavin
Ph: 01.46.33.70.20
or 6 rue du Jour, Paris 1st - <u>métro</u>: Les Halles
Ph: 01.45.08.56.56

3. Kenzo
23 blvd de la Madeleine, Paris 8th - <u>métro</u>: Madeleine
Ph: 01.42.61.04.51
or 60 rue de Rennes, Paris 6th - <u>métro</u>: Rennes
Ph: 01.45.44.27.88

4. Victoire
10/12 place des Victoires, Paris 2nd - <u>métro</u>: Palais Royal
Ph: 01.42.60.96.21

5. Lolita Lempicka
13 bis, rue Pavée, Paris 4th - <u>métro</u>: Saint-Paul
Ph: 01.42.74.50.48

6. Sonia Rykiel
175 blvd St-Germain, Paris 6th - <u>métro</u>: St-Germain-des-Prés
Ph: 01.49.54.60.00

7. Gérard Darel
22 rue Royale, Paris 8th - <u>métro</u>: Madeleine
or 174 blvd St-Germain, Paris 6th - <u>métro</u>: St-Germain-des-Prés
Ph: 01.45.48.54.80

8. Et Vous
25 rue Royale, Paris 8th - <u>métro</u>: Madeleine
Ph: 01.47.42.31.00
or 15 rue des Francs-Bourgeois, Paris 4th - <u>métro</u>: St-Paul
Ph: 01.48.87.48.98

9. Teenflo
18 rue Royale, Paris 8th - <u>métro</u>: Madeleine
Ph: 01.46.60.10.60

10. Irene Van Ryb
53 rue du Four, Paris 6th - <u>métro</u>: Sèvres-Babylone
Ph: 01.42.22.77.17

The Top Ten Men's Wear

1. Kenzo
3 place des Victoires, Paris 2nd - <u>métro</u>: Palais Royal
Ph: 01.40.39.72.00

2. Sonia Rykiel
194 blvd St-Germain, Paris 6th - <u>métro</u>: St-Germain-des-Prés
Ph: 01.49.54.60.00

3. Polo Ralph Lauren
2 place de la Madeleine, Paris 8th - <u>métro</u>: Madeleine
Ph: 01.44.77.53.50

4. Ermenegildo Zegna
10 rue de la Paix, Paris 1st - <u>métro</u>: Opéra
Ph: 01.42.61.67.61

5. Salvatore Ferragamo
50 rue du Faubourg St-Honoré, Paris 8th - <u>métro</u>: Concorde
Ph: 01.43.12.96.96

6. Thierry Mugler
8 Place des Victoires, Paris 2nd - <u>métro</u>: Palais Royal
Ph: 01.49.26.05.02

7. Hugo Boss
374 rue St-Honoré, Paris 1st - <u>métro</u>: Palais Royal
Ph: 01.47.03.40.53

8. Daniel Hechter
146 blvd St-Germain, Paris 6th - <u>métro</u>: Mabillon
Ph: 01.43.26.96.36

9. Façonnable
174 blvd St-Germain, Paris 6th - <u>métro</u>: St-Germain-des-Prés
Ph: 01.40.49.02.47
or 9 rue du Faubourg St-Honoré, Paris 8th - <u>métro</u>: Concorde
Ph: 01.47.42.72.60

10. Harryland
21 rue Pavée, Paris 4th - <u>métro</u>: Saint-Paul
Ph: 01.42.77.53.15

The Top Ten Leather Goods

I. Hermès
24 rue du Faubourg St-Honoré, Paris 8th - <u>métro</u>: Concorde
Ph: 01.40.17.47.17
Although Hermès is known worldwide for its silk scarves and ties, its original specialty was leather.

2. Louis Vuitton
78bis av. Marceau, Paris 8th - <u>métro</u>: George V
Ph: 01.47.20.47.00

3. Goyard
233 rue St-Honoré, Paris 1st - <u>métro</u>: Tuileries
Ph: 01.42.60.57.04

4. Longchamp
390 rue St-Honoré, Paris 1st - <u>métro</u>: Concorde
Ph: 01.42.60.00.00

5. Delvaux
18 rue Royale, Paris 8th - <u>métro</u>: Madeleine
Ph: 01.42.60.85.95

6. Lancel
127 av. des Champs-Elysées, Paris 8th - <u>métro</u>: Franklin D. Roosevelt
Ph: 01.47.23.66.03

7. Morabito
55 rue François 1er, Paris 16th - <u>métro</u>: George V
Ph: 01.53.23.90.40

8. Didier Lamarthe
219 rue St-Honoré, Paris 1st - <u>métro</u>: Tuileries
Ph: 01.42.96.09.90

9. La maroquinerie Parisienne
30 rue Tronchet, Paris 8th - <u>métro</u>: Havre-Caumartin
Ph: 01.47.42.83.40

10. Soco
56 rue Bonaparte, Paris 6th - <u>métro</u>: St-Germain-des-Prés
Ph: 01.40.51.78.76

The Top Ten Jewelry Stores

Paris has some of the most famous jewelry stores in the world. They are all located at place Vendôme and rue de la Paix.

I. Cartier
13 rue de la Paix, Paris 2nd - <u>métro</u>: Opéra or Tuileries
Ph: 01.42.61.58.56
Famous worldwide.

2. Boucheron
26 place Vendôme, Paris 1st - <u>métro</u>: Opéra or Tuileries
Ph: 01.42.61.58.16
An expert in precious stones.

3. Van Cleef & Arpels
22 place Vendôme, Paris 1st - <u>métro</u>: Opéra or Tuileries
Ph: 01.53.45.45.45
Unique jewels worn by the most elegant women, from Maria Callas to Sharon Stone.

4. Chaumet
12 place Vendôme, Paris 1st - <u>métro</u>: Opéra or Tuileries
Ph: 01.44.77.24.00 - Fax: 01.42.60.41.44

5. Mauboussin
20 place Vendôme, Paris 1st - <u>métro</u>: Opéra or Tuileries
Ph: 01.44.55.10.00 - Fax: 01.44.55.10.09

6. Piaget
16 place Vendôme, Paris 1st - <u>métro</u>: Opéra or Tuileries
Ph: 01.42.60.30.44 - Fax: 01.42.60.30.44
A large selection of watches.

7. Bulgari
27 av. Montaigne, Paris 8th - <u>métro</u>: Franklin D. Roosevelt
Ph: 01.53.23.92.92

8. Chanel
18 Place Vendôme, Paris 1st - <u>métro</u>: Opéra or Tuileries
Ph: 01.55.35.50.05
Brand new boutique opened in October 1997.

9. Poiray
1 rue de la Paix, Paris 2nd - <u>métro</u>: Opéra
Ph: 01.42.61.70.58

10. Mellerio dits Meller
1 rue de la Paix, Paris 2nd - <u>métro</u>: Opéra
Ph: 01.42.61.57.53

The Top Ten Tablewares (crystal, china & silver)

Rue Royale, between Concorde and Madeleine, houses the most famous brands of crystal, china, and silver.

1. Christofle
9 rue Royale, Paris 8th - <u>métro</u>: Concorde
Ph: 01.49.33.43.00
Beautiful silver items and china.

2. Cristalleries de Saint-Louis
13 rue Royale, Paris 8th - <u>métro</u>: Concorde
Ph: 01.40.17.01.74
Refinement and elegance characterize this famous crystal boutique.

3. Lalique
11 rue Royale, Paris 8th - <u>métro</u>: Concorde
Ph: 01.53.05.12.12
Very fine crystal.

4. Bernardaud
11 rue Royale, Paris 8th - <u>métro</u>: Concorde
Ph: 01.47.42.88.66
Great collection of china.

5. Daum
4 rue de la Paix, Paris 2nd - <u>métro</u>: Opéra
Ph: 01.42.61.25.25

6. Baccarat
11 place de la Madeleine, Paris 8th - <u>métro</u>: Madeleine
Ph: 01.42.65.36.26

7. Villeroy & Boch
21 rue Royale, Paris 8th - <u>métro</u>: Madeleine or Concorde
Ph: 01.42.65.81.84

8. Odiot
7 place de la Madeleine, Paris 8th - <u>métro</u>: Madeleine
Ph: 01.42.65.00.95
Silversmiths in Paris since 1690.

9. Ercuis
Galerie royale, 9 rue Royale, Paris 8th - <u>métro</u>: Madeleine
Ph: 01.40.17.01.00
High quality silver.

10. Rosenthal
99 rue de Rivoli, Carroussel du Louvre, Paris 1st - <u>métro</u>:
Palais-Royal
Ph: 01.40.20.07.19

The Top Ten Home Décor

I. The Conran Shop
117 rue du Bac, Paris 7th - <u>métro</u>: Sèvres-Babylone
Ph: 01.42.84.10.01
Very trendy.

2. Habitat
Among several locations:
12 blvd de la Madeleine, Paris 9th - <u>métro</u>: Madeleine
Ph: 01.42.68.12.76
45 rue de Rennes, Paris 6th - <u>métro</u>: Rennes
Ph: 01.45.44.68.74
Lovely items at reasonable prices.

3. Manuel Canovas
7 rue de Furstenberg, Paris 6th - <u>métro</u>: Odéon
Ph: 01.43.25.75.98
Beautiful fabrics and wallpapers.

4. Nobilis Fontan
38 rue Bonaparte, Paris 6th - <u>métro</u>: St-Germain-des-Prés
Ph: 01.43.29.12.71

5. Besson
32 rue Bonaparte, Paris 6th - <u>métro</u>: St-Germain-des-Prés
Ph: 01.40.51.89.64

6. Pierre Frey
47 rue des Petits-Champs, Paris 1st - <u>métro</u>: Opéra
Ph: 01.44.77.36.00
International reputation for its fabrics and wall-coverings.

7. Maison de famille
29 rue St-Sulpice, Paris 6th - <u>métro</u>: St-Sulpice
Ph: 01.40.46.97.47

8. Yves Halard
252 blvd Saint-Germain, Paris 6th - <u>métro</u>: Raspail
Ph: 01.42.22.60.50

9. Etamine

63 rue du Bac, Paris 7th - <u>métro</u>: Rue du Bac
Ph: 01.42.22.03.16
Very trendy boutique.

10. Elle

30 rue St-Sulpice, Paris 6th - <u>métro</u>: St-Sulpice.
Ph: 01.43.26.46.10
Items chosen by the editors of "ELLE Décoration".

The Top Ten Beauty Parlors (instituts de beauté)

I. Guerlain
68 av. des Champs-Elysées, Paris 8th - <u>métro</u>: Franklin D. Roosevelt
Ph: 01.45.62.11.21
or 29 rue de Sèvres, Paris 6th - <u>métro</u>: Sèvres-Babylone
Ph: 01.42.22.87.96

2. Carita
18 rue Mesnil, Paris 16th - <u>métro</u>: Victor Hugo
Ph: 01.47.27.18.43

3. Carita International
11 rue du Faubourg St-Honoré, Paris 8th - <u>métro</u>: Concorde
Ph: 01.44.94.11.11

4. Yves Saint Laurent
38 rue du Fbg St-Honoré, Paris 8th - <u>métro</u>: Champs-Elysées-Clémenceau
Ph: 01.42.65.74.59

5. Institut Lancôme
29 rue du Faubourg St-Honoré, Paris 8th - <u>métro</u>: Champs-Elysées-Clémenceau
Ph: 01.42.65.30.74

6. Orlane
163 av. Victor Hugo, Paris 16th - <u>métro</u>: Victor Hugo
Ph: 01.47.04.65.00

7. Institut Clarins
4 rue Berteaux Dumas, 92200 Neuilly sur Seine - <u>métro</u>: Pont-de-Neuilly
Ph: 01.46.24.01.81

8. Institut Matis
26 rue Godot de Mauroy, Paris 9th - <u>métro</u>: Madeline
Ph: 01.47.42.82.03

9. Institut Maria Galland
7 av. Marceau, Paris 16th - <u>métro</u>: Alma-Marceau
Ph: 01.47.20.14.77

10. Alexandre
3 av. Matignon, Paris 8th - <u>métro</u>: Champs-Elysées-
Clémenceau
Ph: 01.42.25.57.90

The Top Ten Artistic Events

I. Fête de la Musique and Summer Solstice celebration
Streets of Paris
Ph: 01.40.03.94.70
June 21.
Live music is performed throughout the streets, cafés and squares of Paris during all night.

2. Festival du Marais
Tickets at: 44 rue François-Miron, Paris 4th - <u>métro</u>: Saint-Paul
Ph: 01.48.87.60.08
From mid-June to mid-July.
Classical and Jazz music, dance and theater are performed in the churches and private mansions of the Marais.

3. Festival d'Art Sacré
Ph: 01.44.70.64.10
From mid-November to mid-December.
Sacred music played in the Conciergerie, in Jacquemart-André museum and in several churches.

4. FIAC (Foire Internationale d'Art Contemporain)
Espace Eiffel Branly
29-55 quai de Branly, Paris 7th - <u>métro</u>: Iéna
Ph: 01.41.90.47.47
In October.
Modern art exhibition.

5. Fête du Cinéma
Late June.
During this special day, with one regular-price ticket you can see as many as movies you want.

6. Journées du Patrimoine
Ph: 01.44.61.21.50
3rd weekend in September.
Free entrance in all national monuments that are normally closed to the public (Sénat, Elysées, Assemblée Nationale...)

7. Musique en l'Ile
In July and August.
Classical music concerts held in the 17th century Eglise Saint-Louis on the Ile Saint-Louis.

8. Musique Baroque au Château de Versailles
From mid-September through mid-October.
Baroque music festival in the beautiful Château de Versailles.

9. La Villette Jazz Festival
La Villette
Ph: 01.40.03.75.03
From Late June to mid-July.

10. Salon du Livre
Parc des Expositions, Porte de Versailles, Paris 15th - métro: Porte de Versailles
Ph: 01.43.95.37.00
In March.
Annual book exhibition.

The Top Ten Places for Classical Music and Opera

I. Salle Pleyel
252 rue du Faubourg St-Honoré, Paris 8th - <u>métro</u>: Ternes
Ph: 01.45.61.53.00
Paris' main home for classical music, hosting the Paris Symphony Orchestra regularly. Hosted Chopin's last public peformance.

2. Opéra Garnier
Place de l'Opéra, Paris 9th - <u>métro</u>: Opéra
Ph: 01.40.01.17.89 - Fax: 01.40.01.25.60
One of the most beautiful theatres in the world. Today it hosts ballets.

3. Opéra Bastille
Place de la Bastille, Paris 11th - <u>métro</u>: Bastille
Ph: 01.47.73.13.00
Today Paris' main opera house.

4. Theâtre des Champs-Elysées
15 av. de Montaigne, Paris 8th - <u>métro</u>: Alma-Marceau
Ph: 01.49.52.50.50
Hosts concerts, ballets and plays.

5. Theâtre du Châtelet
Place du Châtelet, Paris 1st - <u>métro</u>: Châtelet
Ph: 01.40.28.28.40 - Fax: 01.40.28.28.87

6. Cité de la Musique
Parc de la Villette, 221 av. Jean Jaurès, Paris 19th - <u>métro</u>: Porte de Pantin
Ph: 01.44.84.44.84
Many concerts of classical and world music.

7. Sainte Chapelle
4 blvd du Palais, Paris 1st - <u>métro</u>: Cité
Ph: 01.53.73.78.50 - Fax: 01.40.51.70.36

8. Opéra Comique
   5 rue Favart, Paris 2nd - <u>métro</u>: Richelieu-Drouot
   Ph: 01.42.96.12.20
   Comic operas.

9. Eglise Américaine (American Church)
   65 Quai d'Orsay, Paris 7th - <u>métro</u>: Invalides
   Ph: 01.40.62.05.00
   Concerts every Sunday at 6 pm, except in July and August.

10. Eglise Saint-Merri
   78 rue St-Martin, Paris 4th - <u>métro</u>: Hôtel-de-Ville
   Ph: 01.42.71.93.93
   Concerts every Saturday at 9 pm and Sunday at 4 pm, except in August.

The Top Ten Theaters

The Parisian theatrical scene is very important. Check the weekly Paris cultural guide ('Pariscope' or 'Officiel') to choose a play. Here are the capital's best theatres.

I. La Comédie Française
Place André Malraux, Paris 1st - <u>métro</u>: Palais-Royal
Ph: 01.44.58.15.15 - Fax: 01.44.58.15.00
The most classic theatre. If you show up early in the evening you may get cheap last-minute tickets.

2. Théâtre de l'Odéon
Place de l'Odéon, Paris 6th - <u>métro</u>: Odéon
Ph: 01.44.41.36.36 - Fax: 01.44.41.36.01

3. Théâtre Mogador
25 rue de Mogador, Paris 9th - <u>métro</u>: Trinité
Ph: 01.53.32.32.00

4. Théâtre de la Renaissance
20 blvd Saint-Martin, Paris 10th - <u>métro</u>: Strasbourg-St-Denis
Ph: 01.42.08.18.50

5. Café de la Gare
41 rue du Temple, Paris 4th - <u>métro</u>: Rambuteau
Ph: 01.42.78.52.51
A typical Parisian "café-théâtre".

6. Théâtre du Vieux Colombier
21 rue du Vieux Colombier, Paris 6th - <u>métro</u>: St. Sulpice
Ph: 01.44.39.87.00 - Fax: 01.44.39.87.19

7. Théâtre National de Chaillot
1 place du Trocadéro, Paris 16th - <u>métro</u>: Trocadéro
Ph: 01.47.27.81.15 - Fax: 01.47.27.39.23

8. Théâtre Marigny
Carré Marigny, Paris 8th - <u>métro</u>: Champs-Elysées-Clémenceau
Ph: 01.42.76.66.79

9. Théâtre de la Michodière
5 rue La Michodière, Paris 2nd - <u>métro</u>: Bonne Nouvelle
Ph: 01.47.42.95.22

10. Théâtre National de la Colline
15 rue Malte-Brun, Paris 20th - <u>métro</u>: Gambetta
Ph: 01.44.62.52.52 - Fax: 01.44.62.52.90

The Top Ten Jazz Spots

Most jazz clubs are located in the Latin Quarter or around Les Halles.

I. Le Bilboquet
13 rue Saint Benoit, Paris 6th - <u>métro</u>: St-Germain-des-Prés
Ph: 01.45.48.81.84

2. Caveau de la Huchette
5 rue de la Huchette, Paris 5th - <u>métro</u>: Saint-Michel
Ph: 01.43.26.65.05

3. Au Duc des Lombards
42 rue des Lombards, Paris 1st - <u>métro</u>: Les Halles
Ph: 01.42.33.22.88

4. New Morning
7 rue des Petites-Ecuries, Paris 10th - <u>métro</u>: Château d'Eau
Ph: 01.45.23.51.41

5. Lionel Hampton Jazz Club (Le Méridien)
81 blvd Gouvion-St-Cyr, Paris 17th - <u>métro</u>: Porte Maillot
Ph: 01.40.68.30.42

6. Le Montana
28 rue St-Benoit, Paris 6th - <u>métro</u>: St-Germain-des-Prés
Ph: 01.45.48.93.08

7. Le Baiser Salé
58 rue des Lombards, Paris 1st - <u>métro</u>: Les Halles
Ph: 01.42.33.37.71

8. Le Sunset
60 rue des Lombards, Paris 1st - <u>métro</u>: Les Halles
Ph: 01.40.26.46.50

9. La Villa
29 rue Jacob, Paris 6th - <u>métro</u>: St-Germain-des-Prés
Ph: 01.43.26.60.00

10. Le Petit Journal
71 blvd St-Michel, Paris 5th - <u>métro</u>: Saint-Michel or RER
Luxembourg
Ph: 01.43.26.28.59

The Top Ten Pubs

Most pubs are located in the 1st and 2nd arrondissements.
English speakers gather here after work.

I. Kitty O'Shea
10 rue des Capucines, Paris 2nd - <u>métro</u>: Opéra or Madeleine
Ph: 01.40.15.00.30
The meeting place for English speakers working in the area.

2. Flann O'Brien
6 rue Bailleul, Paris 1st - <u>métro</u>: Châtelet or Louvre-Rivoli
Ph: 01.42.60.13.58
One of the very first Irish pubs in Paris.

3. Carr's
1 rue du Mont-Thabor, Paris 1st - <u>métro</u>: Tuileries
Ph: 01.42.60.60.26
Very cozy atmosphere.

4. The Auld Alliance
80 rue François Miron, Paris 4th - <u>métro</u>: Saint-Paul
Ph: 01.48.04.30.40
Scottish pub with beer from Edinburg and Glasgow and a large variety of whisky.

5. The Frog & Rosbif
116 rue Saint-Denis, Paris 2nd - <u>métro</u>: Etienne-Marcel or Les Halles
Ph: 01.42.36.34.73
Make their own beer (brewery on the basement). Very British.

6. Finnegan's Wake
9 rue des Boulangers, Paris 5th - <u>métro</u>: Jussieu or Cardinal
Ph: 01.46.34.23.65
Pleasant atmosphere in this Irish Pub.

7. The Kildare Irish Pub
6bis rue du Quatre-Septembre, Paris 2th - <u>métro</u>: Bourse
Ph: 01.47.03.91.91

8. Tigh Johnny's, The Irish Pub
55 rue Montmartre, Paris 2nd - <u>métro</u>: Etienne-Marcel
Ph: 01.42.33.91.33
Cheapest Guinness in Paris.

9. Quigley's
5 rue du Jour, Paris 1st - <u>métro</u>: Les Halles or Etienne-Marcel
Ph: 01.45.08.17.04
Irish Pub.

10. Connoly's Corner
12 rue de Mirbel, Paris 5th - <u>métro</u>: Censier-Daubenton
Ph: 01.43.31.94.22

The Top Ten Bars

After dinner and before going to a disco, enjoy a few drinks in a trendy bar.

1. Bar Hemingway, Hôtel Ritz
15 place Vendôme, Paris 1st - <u>métro</u>: Opéra or Tuileries
Ph: 01.43.16.30.30
Quiet and elegant bar, worldwide famous. Cocktails: 100F.

2. Le Bar Sans Nom
49 rue de Lappe, Paris 11th - <u>métro</u>: Bastille
Ph: 01.48.05.59.36
The bar "without name" because one day a client called it so. Some of the best cocktails in Paris, in a very nice atmosphere.

3. Villa Barclay
3 av. Matignon, Paris 8th - <u>métro</u>: Franklin D. Roosevelt
Ph: 01.53.89.18.91
Trendy meeting point for the wealthy Parisian youth. Piano bar and disco.

4. La Perla
26 rue François Miron, Paris 4th - <u>métro</u>: Saint-Paul
Ph: 01.42.77.59.40 - Fax: 01.48.87.15.14
The best Mexican bar in Paris.

5. Le Piano Vache
8 rue Laplace, Paris 5th - <u>métro</u>: Maubert-Mutualité
Ph: 01.46.33.75.03
Certainly the place where you'll find the most students.

6. China Club
50 rue de Charenton, Paris 12th - <u>métro</u>: Bastille
Ph: 01.43.43.82.02
Very cozy atmosphere.

7. Les Etages
35 rue Vieille-du-Temple, Paris 4th - <u>métro</u>: Saint-Paul or Hôtel-de-ville
Ph: 01.42.79.72.00
In the heart of the lively Marais.

8. Montecristo Café
   68 av des Champs-Elysées, Paris 8th - <u>métro</u>: Franklin D.
   Roosevelt
   Ph: 01.45.62.30.86 - Fax: 01.45.62.22.76
   *A Cuban café, restaurant, bar and nightclub. Serves Latin
   American specialties.*

9. Café de l'Industrie
   16 rue Saint-Sabin, Paris 11th - <u>métro</u>: Bastille or Bréguet-
   Sabin
   Ph : 01.47.00.13.53
   Crowded every night.

10. Chesterfield Café
   124 rue de la Boétie, Paris 8th - <u>métro</u>: Franklin D. Roosevelt
   Ph: 01.42.25.18.06

The Top Ten Gay & Lesbian Places

The Marais is Paris' main center of gay social life, especially around rue Vieille-du-Temple and rue Sainte-Croix-de-la-Bretonnerie.

1. **Banana Café**
   13 rue de la Ferronnerie, Paris 1st - <u>métro</u>: Châtelet or Les Halles
   Ph: 01.42.33.35.31
   Very trendy address for gays and lesbians. Many stars too.

2. **Le Central**
   33 rue Vieille du Temple, Paris 4th - <u>métro</u>: Hôtel-de-Ville
   Ph: 01.48.87.99.33
   One of the oldest gay bars.

3. **Amnesia Café**
   42 rue Vieille du Temple, Paris 4th- <u>métro</u>: Hôtel-de-Ville
   Ph: 01.42.72.16.94
   Very cozy. For men and women.

4. **Quetzal Bar**
   Rue des Mauvais Garçons / rue de la Verrerie, Paris 4th- <u>métro</u>: Hôtel-de-Ville
   Ph: 01.48.87.99.07
   For men.

5. **Duplex Bar d'Art**
   25 rue Michel Le Comte, Paris 3rd - <u>métro</u>: Rambuteau
   Ph: 01.42.72.80.86

6. **Le Queen**
   102 av. des Champs-Elysées, Paris 8th - <u>métro</u>: Franklin D. Roosevelt
   Ph: 01.53.89.08.90
   Very trendy disco.

7. **Le Piano-Zinc**
   49 rue des Blancs-Manteaux, Paris 4th - <u>métro</u>: Rambuteau or Hôtel-de-ville
   Ph: 01.42.74.32.42

8. La Champmeslé
4 rue Chabanais, Paris 2nd - <u>métro</u>: Pyramides
Ph: 01.42.96.85.20
Cozy club for women.

9. Le Palace Gay Tea Dance
8 rue du Faubourg-Montmartre, Paris 9th - <u>métro</u>: Rue-Montmartre
Ph: 01.42.46.10.87
A large crowd gathers here on Sunday afternoons.

10. Le Privilège
In the basement of the Palace
8 rue du Faubourg-Montmartre, Paris 9th - <u>métro</u>: Rue-Montmartre
Ph: 01.47.70.75.02

The Top Ten Dance Clubs / Discos

I. Les Bains
7 rue du Bourg-l'Abbé, Paris 3rd - <u>métro</u>: Etienne Marcel
Ph: 01.44.54.22.22
Private club where you'll see all the stars. House,techno.
Restaurant inside.

2. Le Queen
102 av. des Champs-Elysées, Paris 8th - <u>métro</u>: Franklin D.
Roosevelt
Ph: 01.53.89.08.90
Gay club, hetero night on Wednesdays. International
reputation.

4. Villa Barclay
3 av. Matignon, Paris 8th - <u>métro</u>: Franklin D. Roosevelt
Ph: 01.53.89.18.91
Very trendy place. Piano-bar and disco.

3. Les Planches
40 rue du Colisée, Paris 8th - <u>métro</u>: St Philippe du Roule
Ph: 01.42.25.11.68
Frequented by the wealthy Parisian youth.

5. La Casbah
20 rue de la Forge-Royale, Paris 11th - <u>métro</u>: Bastille
Ph: 01.43.79.69.04
Beautiful Moroccan décor. Restaurant inside.

7. Le Niel's
27 av. Ternes, Paris 17th - <u>métro</u>: Ternes
Ph: 01.47.66.45.00

6. Le Gibus
18 rue du Faubourg-du-Temple, Paris 11th - <u>métro</u>:
République
Ph: 01.47.00.78.88
Jungle, Hardhouse, Techno, and Transgoa.

8. Le Duplex

2 bis avenue Foch, Paris 16th - <u>métro</u>: Charles de Gaulle-Etoile
Ph: 01.45.00.45.00

9. La Locomotive

90, blvd de Clichy, Paris 18th - <u>métro</u>: Blanche
Ph: 01.53.41.88.88
Many tourists and young people.

10. Le Balajo

9 rue de Lappe, Paris 11th - <u>métro</u>: Bastille
Ph: 01.47.00.07.87
Rock, Cuban, Techno, Disco.

The Top Ten Nightclubs and Cabarets

Some of Paris' cabarets, like the Lido or the Moulin Rouge, have become famous worldwide. Expect to spend around 1,000 F for dinner and show.

I. Lido de Paris
116 bis av. Des Champs-Elysées, Paris 8th - <u>métro</u>: George V
Ph: 01.40.76.56.10 - Fax: 01.45.61.19.41
The most international cabaret with the famous Bluebell Girls.

2. Moulin Rouge
82 blvd de Clichy, Paris 18th - <u>métro</u>: Blanche
Ph: 01.46.06.00.19 - Fax: 01.42.23.02.00
Famous for its French-cancan. Was the favorite place of the painter Toulouse-Lautrec.

3. Crazy Horse
12 av George V, Paris 8th - <u>métro</u>: George V or Alma Marceau
Ph: 01.47.23.32.32 - Fax: 01.47.23.48.26
One of the most erotic cabarets in Paris.

4. Folies Bergère
32 rue Richer, Paris 9th - <u>métro</u>: Rue-Montmartre or Cadet
Ph: 01.44.79.98.98 - Fax: 01.40.22.94.47
Closed on Mondays.

5. Le Paradis Latin
28 rue Cardinal Lemoine, Paris 5th - <u>métro</u>: Jussieu or Cardinal Lemoine
Ph: 01.43.25.28.28 - Fax: 01.43.29.63.63
Closed on Tuesdays.

6. Chez Michou
80 rue des Martyrs, Paris 18th - <u>métro</u>: Pigalle
Ph: 01.46.06.16.04 - Fax: 01.42.64.50.50

7. La Belle Epoque
36 rue des Petits Champs, Paris 2nd - <u>métro</u>: Pyramides
Ph: 01.42.96.33.33 - Fax: 01.49.27.03.42

8. **Nouvelle Eve**
   25 rue Fontaine, Paris 9th - <u>métro</u>: Blanche
   Ph: 01.48.74.69.25 - Fax: 01.42.85.38.27

9. **Villa d'Este**
   4 rue Arsène-Houssaye, Paris 8th - <u>métro</u>: Charles-de-Gaulle-
   Etoile
   Ph: 01.42.56.14.65

10. **Milliardaire**
    68 rue Pierre-Charron, Paris 8th - <u>métro</u>: Franklin D.
    Roosevelt
    Ph: 01.42.89.88.09

The Top Ten Books about Paris

1. **Notre-Dame de Paris -** Victor Hugo

2. **Au Bonheur des Dames -** Emile Zola

3. **Mémoires d'une jeune fille rangée -** Simone de Beauvoir

4. **Bel Ami -** Guy de Maupassant

5. **Le Père Goriot -** Honoré de Balzac

6. **Le ventre de Paris -** Emile Zola

7. **Paris -** Julien Green

8. **La Place de l'Etoile -** Patrick Modiano

9. **Nocturne Parisien -** Paul Verlaine

10. **La Fée Carabine -** Daniel Pennac

The Top Ten Songs about Paris

1. **Il est cinq heures, Paris s'éveille** - Jacques Dutronc

2. **Le poinçonneur des lilas** - Serge Gainsbourg

3. **Les Champs-Elysées** - Joe Dassin

4. **Sous le ciel de Paris** - Edith Piaf

5. **Les prénoms de Paris** - Jacques Brel

6. **Pont Mirabeau** - Léo Ferré

7. **Paris Canaille** - Juliette Gréco

8. **Comme ils disent** - Charles Aznavour

9. **Le bateau-mouche** - Alain Souchon

10. **Revoir Paris** - Charles Trénet

The Top Ten Movies about Paris

1. **Hôtel du Nord (1938) -** Marcel Carné

2. **Le Dernier Métro (1980) -** François Truffaut

3. **Chacun Cherche son Chat (1996) -** Cédric Klapisch

4. **Les Enfants du Paradis (1955) -** Marcel Carné

5. **Last Tango in Paris (1972) -** Bernardo Bertolluci

6. **La Passante du Sans Souci (1981) -** Jacques Rouffio

7. **A Bout de Souffle (1959) -** Jean-Luc Godard

8. **Les 400 Coups (1959) -** François Truffaut

9. **Subway (1985) -** Luc Besson

10. **Un Monde Sans Pitié (1989) -** Eric Rochant

The Top Ten Pulses of the City

1.	6am	Starts to come to life.
2.	7am	Trash is collected, fresh food is delivered.
3.	9am	Office workers start pouring into business center and commercial business starts.
4.	10am	Stores and museums open.
5.	1pm	Office workers meet at cafés or restaurants for one-hour lunch break.
6.	6pm	Rush hour in the metro.
7.	8pm	Dinner eaten at home.
8.	9pm	Dinner eaten out.
9.	11pm	People head for home (weekdays).
10.	1am	People head for home (weekends).

The Top Ten Business Sites

I. La Défense
With its modern high-rise buildings, La Défense is THE business district. Most large companies are located here, including Total, Elf, Société Générale.

2. Opéra
Most banks have their headquarters around Opéra square (BNP blvd Haussmann, Crédit Lyonnais blvd des Italiens, Paribas rue d'Antin, JP Morgan place Vendôme).

3. Rungis
The Paris market left Les Halles district in 1969 and moved to Rungis, in the south of Paris. Today all the food travels through Rungis, an enormous market place where the activity starts every day at 5 am.

4. Champs-Elysées
Advertising agencies, banks, and luxury companies.

5. La Bourse
The stock market district.

6. Avenue Charles de Gaulle - Neuilly
Procter & Gamble, Deloitte & Touche and many other companies are located here, between the Champs-Elysées and La Défense.

7. Avenue Montaigne and Rue du Faubourg St-Honoré
Haute Couture boutiques.

8. Rue du temple (Paris 3rd)
Diamonds and gold.

9. Le Sentier (Paris 2nd and 3rd)
Fabrics and clothes.

10. St-Germain-des-Prés
Quality antiques.

The Top Ten Brand Names

1. **Chanel**
   The French haute couture par excellence.

2. **Dior**
   Another famous name for haute couture and cosmetics.

3. **Evian**
   The world famous mineral water!

4. **Hermès**
   The symbol of Parisian chic (leather, clothes, accessories, jewels, china).

5. **Perrier**
   The famous sparkling water.

6. **Moët & Chandon**
   The most famous champagne.

7. **L'Oréal**
   Cosmetics.

8. **Michelin**
   The king of the French tire.

9. **Salomon**
   Skis and boots sold everywhere in the world.

10. **Bic**
    The most famous pen in the world.

The Top Ten Trips outside Paris

I. Versailles
Visitor information at 7 rue des Réservoirs
Ph: 01.39.50.36.22
Closed on Mondays.
The "Château de Versailles" housed several generations of French royalty. Its history began when Louis XIV transformed his father's hunting lodge into a palace of unimaginable opulence. Don't miss the splendid Hall of Mirrors (where the famous Treaty of Versailles was signed), the king's chambers and the queen's apartments, and the beautiful gardens with their elaborate fountains.

2. The Gardens of Giverny
80km northwest from Paris.
Ph: 02.32.51.28.21
From April to October, Tues-Sun, 10 am - 6 pm.
From 1883 to 1926, the impressionist Claude Monet painted his most famous works in the gardens of Giverny.

3. Chantilly
45km north of Paris.
Château de Chantilly (Chantilly's castle)
Ph: 01.44.57.08.00
Wed-Mon 10 am - 6 pm (Nov-Feb 10.30 am - 12.45 pm and 2 pm - 5pm).
Beautiful gardens and many superb paintings.
Musée Vivant du Cheval (Living Horse Museum)
Ph: 01.44.57.40.40
Wed-Mon 10.30 am - 5.30 pm.
Don't miss the magnificent "Grandes Ecuries" (stables) next to Chantilly's famous "Champ de course" (racecourse).

4. Cathédrale Notre-Dame de Chartres
Tourist office at 16 Cloitre Notre-Dame.
Ph: 02.37.21.75.02
Open daily from 7.30 am to 7 pm.
A 50 minute ride by train from gare Montapnasse
Magnificent gothic cathedral built in the 13th century.

5. Château de Vaux-le-Vicomte
77950 Maincy
Ph: 01.64.14.41.90
Don't miss the candlelight evenings every Saturday from 8.30 pm to 11 pm (from May to mid-October).

6. Château et Forêt de Fontainebleau
Visitor information at 31 place Napoléon-Bonaparte
Ph: 01.64.22.25.68

7. Saint-Germain-en-Laye
Office de Tourisme: 38 rue au Pain
Ph: 01.34.51.05.12
Access: RER line A1
St-Germain-en-Laye is a wealthy Parisian suburb that looks like a provincial town. Its castle was transformed by Napoleon III into a museum of antiquity: Musée des Antiquités Nationales (ph: 01.34.51.53.65).

8. Loire Valley
The Loire Valley, in the middle of French countryside, is known as the playground of the Kings. Among the most beautiful châteaux: the large and gorgeous Château Chambord, the lovely renaissance Azay-le-Rideau, and the Château de Chenonceau, an architectural wonder straddling the river Cher.

9. Mont-Saint-Michel
Office de Tourisme de la Baie du Mont St-Michel
3bis grande rue des Stuarts 35120 Dol-de-Bretagne
Ph: 02.99.48.34.53
A great natural site.

10. The D-Day landing beaches in Normandy
250km northwest of Paris.
Comité Régional de Tourisme de Normandie
14 rue Charles Corbeau 72000 Evreux
Ph: 02.32.33.79.00 - Fax: 02.32.31.19.04 - e-mail:
info@normandy-tourism.org
A very interesting trip to immerse oneself in World War II history. Do not miss the impressive American cemetery overlooking Omaha Beach, the Pointe-du-Hoc, Ste-Mère Eglise, and the history museum at Arromanches.

Phrases

The Top Ten Most Important Phrases You Must Know

1.	**Yes**	Oui
2.	**No**	Non
3.	**Hello - Good morning/ Good afternoon**	Bonjour
4.	**Goodbye**	Au revoir
5.	**Please**	S'il vous plaît
6.	**Thank you**	Merci
7.	**You're welcome**	Je vous en prie
8.	**Excuse me**	Excusez-moi
9.	**Sorry**	Désolé / Pardon
10.	**Where is...?**	Où est...?

The Top Ten Phrases if You Don't Understand French

1. **Please excuse my poor French.**
   Veuillez excuser mon mauvais français.

2. **Do you speak English?**
   Parlez-vous anglais?

3. **I can't speak French.**
   Je ne parle pas français.

4. **I don't understand.**
   Je ne comprends pas.

5. **How do you say... in French?**
   Comment dit-on... en français?

6. **Could you please spell it?**
   Est-ce que vous pouvez l'épeler?

7. **Could you please write that down?**
   Est-ce que vous pouvez l'écrire?

8. **Could you please repeat slowly?**
   Est-ce que vous pouvez répéter lentement?

9. **Could you please translate this?**
   Est-ce que vous pouvez me traduire ceci?

10. **Do you have a dictionary English-French?**
    Avez-vous un dictionnaire anglais-français?

The Top Ten Phrases for Meeting People

1. **My name is...**
   Je m'appelle...

2. **What is your name?**
   Comment vous appelez-vous? (formal)
   Comment t'appelles-tu? (informal)

3. **Pleased to meet you**
   Enchanté(e) / Très heureux (se).

4. **How are you?**
   Comment allez-vous? (formal)
   Comment vas-tu? (informal)

5. **Where are you from?**
   D'où venez-vous?
   D' où viens-tu?

6. **I'm from...**
   Je viens de...

7. **Do you live in Paris?**
   Est-ce que vous habitez à Paris?
   Est-ce que tu habites à Paris?

8. **Could we get together while I am here?**
   Pourrions-nous nous voir pendant que je suis ici?

9. **My telephone number is ...**
   Mon numéro de téléphone est le ...

10. **I will call you.**
    Je vous appellerai / je t'appellerai.

The Top Ten Most Important Signs You Will See

1.	**Ladies**	Dames
2.	**Gentlemen**	Messieurs
3.	**Elevator**	Ascenseur
4.	**Stairs**	Escaliers
5.	**Push**	Poussez
6.	**Pull**	Tirez
7.	**Exit**	Sortie
8.	**Emergency exit**	Sortie de secours
9.	**Do not enter**	Interdit
10.	**No smoking**	Interdit de fumer

The Top Ten Emergency Phrases

1. **Help!**
   A l'aide!
   Au secours!

2. **I need help.**
   J'ai besoin d'aide.

3. **It's an emergency!**
   C'est une urgence!

4. **Call the Police.**
   Appelez la police.

5. **Get me the Police.**
   Allez me chercher la police.

6. **It hurts.**
   J'ai mal.

7. **I need to get to a hospital.**
   Je dois aller à l'hôpital.

8. **I need a doctor.**
   Il me faut un médecin.

9. **I need an ambulance.**
   Il me faut une ambulance.

10. **I have been attacked.**
    J'ai été attaqué(e).

The Top Ten Medical Phrases

1. **I feel very sick.**
   Je me sens très malade.

2. **Please get me a doctor.**
   Appelez-moi un docteur s'il vous plaît.

3. **Do you have any aspirins?**
   Avez-vous de l'aspirine?

4. **I have a temperature.**
   J'ai de la température.

5. **I am allergic to...**
   Je suis allergique à...

6. **My stomach is upset.**
   J'ai mal à l'estomac.

7. **I have a headache.**
   J'ai mal à la tête.

8. **Should I go to a hospital?**
   Est-ce que je dois aller à l'hôpital?

9. **How do I get to a hospital?**
   Comment est-ce que je vais à l'hôpital?

10. **Where is the nearest pharmacy?**
    Où se trouve la pharmacie la plus proche?

The Top Ten Telephone Phrases

1. Hello
Allo

2 Who is calling?
De la part de qui?

3. Hold on.
Ne quittez pas.

4. Just a minute.
Un instant.

5. May I speak to...?
Pourrais-je parler à...?

6. He / She is on the line.
Il / Elle est en ligne.

7. Do you want to wait?
Voulez-vous patienter?

8. I do not speak French. Do you speak English?
Je ne parle pas français. Parlez-vous anglais?

9. Can I leave him/her a message?
Est-ce que je peux lui laisser un message?

10. I will call back later.
Je rappellerai plus tard.

The Top Ten Celebration Phrases

	English	French
1.	**Cheers (American Toast)!**	A votre santé!
2.	**Happy Birthday!**	Joyeux Anniversaire!
3.	**Congratulations!**	Félicitations!
4.	**Great!**	Super!
5.	**Wonderful!**	Formidable!
6.	**Merry Christmas!**	Joyeux Noël!
7.	**Happy New Year!**	Bonne Année!
8.	**Happy holidays!**	Bonnes vacances!
9.	**Good luck!**	Bonne chance!
10.	**Excellent!**	Excellent!

The Top Ten Gracious Phrases

1. **Thank you.**
   Merci.

2. **Thanks a lot.**
   Merci beaucoup

3. **Thank you so much.**
   Merci infiniment.

4. **It is so kind of you.**
   C'est très gentil de votre part.

5. **Thank you for your hospitality.**
   Merci pour votre hospitalité.

6. **Thank you for your help.**
   Merci pour votre aide.

7. **I'd like to thank you.**
   Je vous remercie.

8. **Thanks a lot for the wonderful meal.**
   Merci beaucoup pour ce délicieux repas.

9. **You have a lovely family.**
   Vous avez / tu as une famille formidable.

10. **You look very nice.**
    Vous êtes / tu es resplendissant(e).

The Top Ten Numbers

1.	**One**	Un
2.	**Two**	Deux
3.	**Three**	Trois
4.	**Four**	Quatre
5.	**Five**	Cinq
6.	**Six**	Six
7.	**Seven**	Sept
8.	**Eight**	Huit
9.	**Nine**	Neuf
10.	**Ten**	Dix

The Top Ten Time Terms

When speaking, French people use both the 24-hour time system and the a.m./p.m. system. All time schedules are on the 24-hour system.

1. **What time is it?**
   Quelle heure est-il?

2. **It is two a.m.**
   Il est deux heures du matin.

3. **It is two p.m.**
   Il est quatorze heures / Il est deux heures de l'après-midi.

4. **It is half past three.**
   Il est trois heures et demie. / Il est quinze heures trente.

5. **It is noon / midnight.**
   Il est midi / minuit.

6. **In the morning / in the afternoon**
   Le matin / l'après-midi

7. **This morning / This afternoon / Tonight**
   Ce matin / Cet après-midi / Ce soir

8. **At what time do you close / open?**
   A quelle heure est-ce que vous fermez / ouvrez?

9. **I will be there at ...**
   Je serai là à ...

10. **I am sorry for being late.**
    Je suis désolé(e) d'être en retard.

The Top Ten Days

I.	**Monday**	Lundi
2.	**Tuesday**	Mardi
3.	**Wednesday**	Mercredi
4.	**Thursday**	Jeudi
5.	**Friday**	Vendredi
6.	**Saturday**	Samedi
7.	**Sunday**	Dimanche
8.	**Today**	Aujourd'hui
9.	**Tomorrow**	Demain
10.	**This weekend**	Ce week-end

The Top Ten Months (plus two)

1. **January**   Janvier

2. **February**   Février

3. **March**   Mars

4. **April**   Avril

5. **May**   Mai

6. **June**   Juin

7. **July**   Juillet

8. **August**   Août

9. **September**   Septembre

10. **October**   Octobre

11. **November**   Novembre

12. **December**   Décembre

The Top Ten Direction Phrases

1. **On the right**
   A droite

2. **On the Left**
   A gauche

3. **Straight ahead**
   Tout droit

4. **Turn**
   Tournez

5. **Is it far from here?**
   C'est loin d'ici?

6. **Is it within walking distance?**
   Peut-on y aller à pied?

7. **Where is the nearest subway station?**
   Où se trouve la station de métro la plus proche?

8. **I am looking for ...**
   Je cherche ...

9. **Could you tell me where is ...**
   Pouvez-vous m'indiquer où se trouve ...

10. **What is the shortest way to go ...?**
    Quel est le chemin le plus court pour aller ... ?

The Top Ten Reference Points

1.	**Avenue**	Avenue
2.	**Boulevard**	Boulevard
3.	**Street**	Rue
4.	**Square**	Place
5.	**North / South**	Nord / Sud
6.	**West / East**	Ouest / Est
7.	**City center**	Centre ville
8.	**In the suburbs**	Dans la banlieue
9.	**I am at...**	Je suis à ...
10.	**Where is ...**	Où est ...

The Top Ten Types of Stores

1.	**Pharmacy**	Pharmacie
2.	**Food store**	Magasin d'alimentation / Epicerie
3.	**Department store**	Grand magasin
4.	**Men's clothing store**	Magasin de vêtements pour hommes
5.	**Women's clothing store**	Magasin de vêtements pour femmes
6.	**Bookstore**	Librairie
7.	**Bakery**	Boulangerie
8.	**Pastries shop**	Pâtisserie
9.	**Flower store**	Fleuriste
10.	**Caterer**	Traiteur

The Top Ten Shopping Phrases

I. How much?
Combien?

2. It's too expensive.
C'est trop cher.

3. Do you have anything less expensive?
Avez-vous quelque chose de moins cher?

4. Do you have anything about 100 francs?
Avez-vous quelque chose dans les 100 francs?

5. Do you have it in other colors?
Est-ce que vous l'avez dans d'autres couleurs?

6. Do you have it in my size?
Est-ce que vous l'avez dans ma taille?

7. Would you please giftwrap it?
Pouvez-vous faire un paquet cadeau s'il vous plaît?

8. Do you take credit cards?
Est-ce que vous acceptez les cartes de crédit?

9. Do you take traveler checks?
Est-ce que vous acceptez les chèques de voyage?

10. I need a receipt please.
J'ai besoin d'un reçu s'il vous plaît.

The Top Ten Colors

1.	**Black**	Noir
2.	**White**	Blanc
3.	**Blue**	Bleu
4.	**Green**	Vert
5.	**Red**	Rouge
6.	**Yellow**	Jaune
7.	**Pink**	Rose
8.	**Brown**	Marron
9.	**Orange**	Orange
10.	**Beige**	Beige

The Top Ten Fruits

1.	**Apple**	Pomme
2.	**Orange**	Orange
3.	**Strawberries**	Fraises
4.	**Grapes**	Raisin
5.	**Pineapple**	Ananas
6.	**Pear**	Poire
7.	**Cherries**	Cerises
8.	**Peach**	Pêche
9.	**Banana**	Banane
10.	**Raspberries**	Framboises

The Top Ten Vegetables

1.	**Potatoes**	Pommes de terre
2.	**Green beans**	Haricots verts
3.	**Tomatoes**	Tomates
4.	**Eggplants**	Aubergines
5.	**Zucchini**	Courgettes
6.	**Lettuce**	Laitue
7.	**Mushrooms**	Champignons
8.	**Green peas**	Petits pois
9.	**Asparagus**	Asperges
10.	**Spinach**	Epinards

The Top Ten Train Travel Phrases

I. I'd like a one-way / return ticket
Je voudrais un billet aller simple / aller retour

2. Do I need to change trains?
Est-ce que je dois changer de train?

3. What time does the next train leave?
A quelle heure part le prochain train?

4. First / second class
Première / seconde classe

5. Platform
Le quai

6. Ticket
Le billet

7. Smoking / Non smoking
Fumeur / Non fumeur

8. Which track is it on? "Track 20"
Sur quelle voie se trouve le train? "Voie 20".

9. Is this seat free / taken?
Est-ce que cette place est libre / occupée?

10. I'm afraid this is my seat.
C'est ma place.

The Top Ten Airline Travel Phrases

I. When is the next flight to ?
Quand part le prochain avion pour ?

2. A direct flight
Un vol direct

3. Where is luggage pick up?
Où recupère-t-on ses bagages?

4. I'd like a window / an aisle.
Je voudrais une fenêtre / une allée.

5. Which gate is it at? "Gate 12".
A quelle porte dois-je aller? "Porte 12".

6. Which way to gate 12?
Comment puis-je me rendre à la porte 12?

7. My suitcase is lost.
J'ai perdu ma valise.

8. How long will the flight be delayed?
L'avion aura un retard de combien?

9. Baggage check.
Enregistrement des bagages.

10. Where can I confirm the return flight?
Où dois-je confirmer le vol retour?

The Top Ten Auto Terms

I. **Gas / Oil for engine**
L'essence / L'huile pour le moteur

2. **Unleaded**
Sans plomb

3. **Fill it up, please.**
Le plein, s'il vous plaît.

4. **Please check the oil / tires.**
Pouvez-vous vérifier le niveau d'huile / la pression des pneus?

5. **My car has broken down.**
Je suis en panne.

6. **The car will not start.**
La voiture ne démarre pas.

7. **Where is the nearest garage, please?**
Où se trouve le garage le plus proche?

8. **I need a tow.**
J'ai besoin d'une dépanneuse.

9. **I have had an accident.**
J'ai eu un accident.

10. **We need to do a report.**
Nous devons faire un constat.

The Top Ten Phrases when Travelling Together

1.	**My friend**	Mon ami / mon copain
2.	**My boyfriend**	Mon ami
3.	**My girlfriend**	Mon amie
4.	**My wife**	Mon épouse / ma femme
5.	**My husband**	Mon époux / mon mari
6.	**My son**	Mon fils
7.	**My daughter**	Ma fille
8.	**My mother**	Ma mère
9.	**My father**	Mon père
10.	**My family**	Ma famille

The Top Ten Hotel Phrases

1. **I'd like a single / double room.**
   Je voudrais une chambre simple / double.

2. **With shower and toilet**
   Avec douche et WC

3. **With bath and toilet**
   Avec bains et WC

4. **On the street / on the yard**
   Sur la rue / sur cour

5. **Do you have any rooms available?**
   Est-ce que vous avez des chambres libres?

6. **Is breakfast included in the price?**
   Est-ce que le petit-déjeuner est inclus dans le prix?

7. **At what time is breakfast served?**
   A quelle heure est servi le petit déjeuner?

8. **Could you please wake me up tomorrow at...?**
   Pouvez-vous me réveiller demain à...?

9. **I'm sorry, it's too small / too noisy.**
   Je regrette, mais elle est trop petite / trop bruyante.

10. **Can you show me another room?**
    Pouvez-vous me montrer une autre chambre?

The Top Ten Restaurant Phrases

1. **I'd like a table for five.**
   J'aimerais une table pour cinq personnes.

2. **I'd like to reserve a table for tonight.**
   J'aimerais réserver une table pour ce soir.

3. **The check, please.**
   L'addition, s'il vous plaît.

4. **Is service included?**
   Est-ce que le service est compris?

5. **I would like to see the menu.**
   Je voudrais voir la carte.

6. **I'll have the fixed price menu.**
   Je prendrai le menu.

7. **Rare / medium / well done.**
   Saignant / à point / bien cuit.

8. **I am vegetarian.**
   Je suis végétarien(ne).

9. **I'd like to order.**
   J'aimerais commander.

10. **Where are the restrooms?**
    Où sont les toilettes?

The Top Ten Things on a Menu

I.	**Starter**	Entrée
2.	**Main course / Entree**	Plat principal
3.	**Cheese**	Fromages
4.	**Dessert**	Dessert
5.	**Beef**	Boeuf
6.	**Poultry**	Volaille
7.	**Fish**	Poisson
8.	**Seafood**	Crustacés
9.	**Beverages**	Boissons
10.	**Ice cream**	Glaces

The Top Ten Wine Phrases

I.	**Red / white wine**	Vin rouge / blanc
2.	**I'd like a glass of...**	Je voudrais un verre de...
3.	**I'd like a bottle of...**	Je voudrais une bouteille de...
4.	**Champagne**	Champagne
5.	**The wine list**	La carte des vins
6.	**Which wine do you suggest?**	Quel vin nous conseillez-vous?
7.	**A carafe**	Une carafe
8.	**A half bottle**	Une demi-bouteille
9.	**A drink before dinner**	Un apéritif
10.	**A liqueur**	Un digestif / une liqueur

The Top Ten Beverages

I. **Coffee black / with milk /with lots of milk**
    Café noir / crème / au lait

2. **Tea (lemon / sugar)**   Thé (citron / sucre)

3. **Hot chocolate**   Chocolat chaud

4. **Herbal tea**   Tisane

5. **Beer (from the tap)**   Bière (à la pression)

6. **Fruit juice**   Jus de fruit

7. **Mineral water**   Eau minérale

8. **Carbonated / not carbonated** Gazeuse /Plate

9. **Milk**   Lait

10. **Tap water**   Eau du robinet

The Top Ten Phrases for Asking for / Declining a Meeting

1. **A meeting**
   Une réunion

2. **Could I schedule a meeting with you?**
   Est-ce que je pourrais organiser une réunion avec vous?

3. **I would like to discuss this matter further.**
   J'aimerais discuter un peu plus de ce point.

4. **Would Thursday at 3pm be good for you?**
   Est-ce que jeudi à 15 heures vous irait?

5. **I will see you at your office.**
   A bientôt à votre bureau.

6. **I am sorry, but I have to cancel our meeting.**
   Je suis désolé(e), mais je dois annuler notre réunion.

7. **Could we reschedule it for another time?**
   Pourrions-nous la reporter à une autre date?

8. **I am afraid that time is not possible.**
   Je crains que cette date ne soit pas possible.

9. **I will get back to you to confirm.**
   Je vous rappellerai pour confirmer.

10. **I look forward to seeing you.**
    Je suis pressé(e) de vous voir.

The Top Ten Phrases for Asking for / Declining a Date

1. **A date**
   Un rendez-vous

2. **Are you free tonight / this weekend?**
   Es-tu libre ce soir / ce week-end?

3. **Would you like to go out tonight / this weekend?**
   Veux-tu sortir ce soir / ce week-end?

4. **Would you like to go to dinner?**
   Veux-tu aller diner?

5. **Would you like to go to the movies?**
   Veux-tu aller au cinéma?

6. **Would you like to go for a walk?**
   Veux-tu qu'on aille se promener?

7. **I'll pick you up at eight o'clock.**
   Je viens te chercher à huit heures.

8. **I am sorry, but I have to cancel our date.**
   Je suis désolé(e), mais je dois annuler notre rendez-vous.

9. **I will give you a call later.**
   Je t'appellerai plus tard.

10. **I will talk to you later.**
    A bientôt.

The Top Ten Phrases of Love and Affection

1. **I love you.**
   Je t'aime.

2. **Do you love me?**
   Est-ce que tu m'aimes?

3. **I missed you a lot.**
   Tu m'as beaucoup manqué.

4. **I think of you all the time.**
   Je pense à toi tout le temps.

5. **You are beautiful tonight.**
   Tu es superbe ce soir.

6. **I want to stay with you.**
   Je veux rester avec toi.

7. **I don't want to leave.**
   Je ne veux pas partir.

8. **I don't want you to leave.**
   Je ne veux pas que tu partes.

9. **Ask me all that you want.**
   Demande-moi tout ce que tu veux.

10. **I want to marry you.**
    Je veux me marier avec toi.

Maps

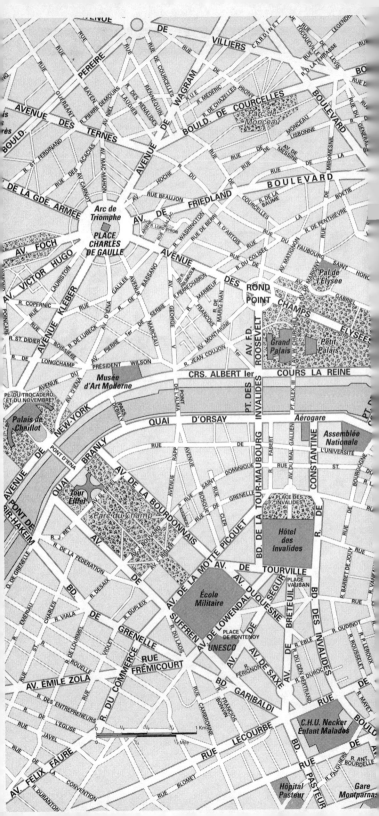